ABOUT THE AUTHOR

Award-winning writer Julia Cameron is the author of
twenty-one books, fiction and nonfiction, including
The Artist's Way, *The Vein of Gold* and *Walking in This
World*. A novelist, playwright, songwriter and poet, she
has extensive credits in theatre, film and television.

LETTERS

to a

YOUNG ARTIST

*Building a Life
in Art*

J U L I A   C A M E R O N

R

RIDER

London · Sydney · Auckland · Johannesburg

1 3 5 7 9 10 8 6 4 2

Copyright © 2005 by Julia Cameron

Julia Cameron has asserted her right to be identified as the author of this work
in accordance with the Copyright, Designs and Patents Act, 1988.

First published in 2005 by Jeremy P. Tarcher,
an imprint of Penguin Putnam Inc., USA.
This edition published in 2005 by Rider,
an imprint of Ebury Press, Random House,
20 Vauxhall Bridge Road, London SW1V 2SA
www.randomhouse.co.uk

Random House Australia (Pty) Limited
20 Alfred Street, Milsons Point, Sydney,
New South Wales 2061, Australia

Random House New Zealand Limited
18 Poland Road, Glenfield,
Auckland 10, New Zealand

Random House South Africa (Pty) Limited
Endulini, 5A Jubilee Road,
Parktown 2193, South Africa

The Random House Group Limited Reg. No. 954009

Most Rider books are available at special quantity discounts for bulk
purchase for sales promotions, premiums, fund-raising, and educational needs.
Special books or book excerpts also can be created to fit specific needs.
For details, write to Rider Special Sales, Random House,
20 Vauxhall Bridge Road, London SW1V 2SA.

BOOK DESIGN BY AMANDA DEWEY

Papers used by Rider are natural, recyclable products
made from wood grown in sustainable forests.

Printed and bound in Great Britain by
Cox & Wyman Ltd, Reading, Berkshire

A CIP catalogue record for this book is available from the British Library

ISBN 1844135594

To Ben Lively,
for building a life in art.

LETTERS

to a

YOUNG ARTIST

Dear X,

I received your letter and I am willing to honor your request for a "connection." In fact, I might enjoy it. I will refrain from asking you questions about your doubtless still fascinating mother. (Although I have a more than mild suspicion that she might have put you up to this whole idea.) You yourself raise interesting questions and I will try to deal with them one at a time. I think I might enjoy answering your questions—if I can, that is. I warn you, some questions can be answered only by personal experience. Then again, when I was your age I wanted shortcuts too. To be honest, I still want shortcuts, but I have learned to do without them.

So where were we?

I think I am probably an immediate disappointment. As a young artist, you have written to me as an older artist, and from your letter I have the creeping suspicion that you think a personal contact with me would "make all the difference." While that is an ego-gratifying notion, it is not the truth as I know it. No one person holds your answers; the world does. (You see, no doubt, that I am putting the responsibility for your life squarely back on you.)

Your answers can come from anywhere, anytime, and, believe me, they will. Therefore, you have to be alert. To be an artist, you can't walk through life watching your own inner movie. If you do that, you might miss something, and that something might be important.

This earth is an interesting place, crammed with people, places, and things that can wake you up and be the spark for a piece of art. You do yourself a grave disservice, even a catastrophic one, if you closet yourself away in the name of Art. Are you doing that? I await your reply.

Dear X,

So you are closeted away in the name of Art. You write that you thought all serious artists needed to be "focused on their work." Yes, up to a point, but that point does not extend to navel gazing. You write that you are trying to avoid "having to take a day job." Well, that's too bad. Your day job may just give you your next novel.

From your letter, I gather you live alone in a studio apartment. It is "modern," you say, and so I take it to be without charm. Of course, as a young person, you may not want charm. You might enjoy Plexiglas cubes for tables for all I know. On my last book tour, I checked into a terrifying hotel filled with such "youthful" decor—neon-orange furniture and the aforementioned cubes. I was told it was very "hip."

Are you "hip"? Isn't hip a bit sterile?

Do I sound like an old bigot? Perhaps I am. It just seems to me that living spaces that are too Zen may not have too much life in them. I am not sure life thrives on minimalism. Mine certainly hasn't, but that's mine.

I have another question for you. Do you believe being an artist involves looking like one? I have had some of my best ideas in pajamas—and they were not basic black or even gray. (I am told gray is the new black. Do you wear it?) I seem to be developing as lively a curiosity about you as you have about me.

Dear X,

Your letter defends what you refer to as your "lifestyle." You do wear black. You are acquiring more gray, and both colors, or noncolors, "make you feel more like an artist."

One of the best writers I know, with the most original mind, looks like a suburban housewife. She's slightly on the plump side; her hair is cut in a no-nonsense bob, and when I was at her house for Thanksgiving, she wore an apron and probably resembled your mother. She is also, I might add, a creditable cook, although it is her prose that is actually delicious. My point is, I have never seen her in black, but I do know she writes every morning. She tells me she averages a page a day, which makes 365 pages in a year and accounts for her novels appearing so regularly. In other words, she has work habits and those are the spine of her artist's identity—not being "hip," not wearing black or gray. She works at her art every day. Do you?

Beware of putting too much effort and energy into "looking" like an artist and too little into making art itself.

Dear X,

I guess I made you mad. Sometimes a bottom-line question can do that. You write that my question about daily productivity made you feel cornered. What's wrong with being cornered? I find it very useful. As a young writer, deadlines—and rent—helped guarantee that I did produce *something*. Over time, the habit of producing became more ingrained. I learned to answer the question "Am I a real artist?" with "Did I make any art today?"

I began to learn that I didn't need to be in the mood to make art in order to make some. Moods were elusive, misleading—and just plain hard to pin down. I exhausted myself waiting for inspiration when I could have simply been working. Furthermore, I learned that my "mood" was an unreliable guide. My negative mood would often tell me good work was "bad." My euphoric mood would tell me bad work was "good." Over time I learned I had to just put in days at the page and sort it out later. I had to learn to be willing to write "badly" some days and to write anyhow. (More on this thought later.)

Are you willing to make art badly?

Somehow I picture you there in your minimalist apartment in search of the "perfect" idea for a "perfect" piece of art that will yield you a "perfect" bull's-eye in your career. I imagine you searching for the precise idea that will "rocket you to the top," make you "hot," give you Andy Warhol's fifteen minutes of fame. Speaking for myself, I want more from life than fifteen minutes in the limelight. I want the daily satisfaction of a job well done, track laid for the day. (Like the early railroad forgers, I want to feel I have laid a certain amount of track each day.)

Lay any track today, buster?

Dear X,

You ask me what is the possible value of bad art? This is a very interesting question. For one thing, we sometimes have to make "bad" art to get to the other side. An artist's growth does not look like a graph ascending straight upward. (Graphs like that belong to real estate fraud.) No, an artist's growth proceeds more sporadically. We make art at a certain level of a certain kind—in a certain style—and then that style collapses. It falls apart. We have outgrown it. It no longer supports us. And so we enter a period of tangled artistic syntax in which we do make art "badly."

I have written entire books in periods where I was writing badly. Those "bad" books got me to the other side. Eventually I wrote well again and better books arose from the ashes of my syntactical hash. Over time I had a body of work, and some parts of that body were "buff," in your phrase, and others were not so buff but equally necessary to the whole body of work. (A misshapen artistic leg can still be used to walk on.)

Many artists quit the first time they hit a "bad" spell. If we think we always have to make "good" art, then when we hit a hard patch we don't work through it. We skid to a halt. We think, "What's this about? Maybe I don't really have a vocation. Maybe I was just deluded, having visions of grandiosity. I'm no real artist. . . ."

Artists of all stripes suffer this mentality, but I will stick to writers, the tribe I know best. The first book is good and the second book maybe not so good, and perhaps the reviews say so in some rather nasty terms, and that hurts, hurts badly, and the writer quits. Gives up. Gives in. Says, "Maybe I wasn't a writer after all."

Now, I want you to notice something. His actual writing talent had nothing to do with this decision; his temperament did. He just wasn't stubborn enough. On the other hand, if the writer keeps writing, maybe the third book is good, the fourth, the fifth, not the sixth, again the seventh good, maybe the eighth. A career is not all home runs. A career is also a lot of base hits that add up to the ball game.

You wrote that you were tearing a lot of things up. I wonder about such snap judgments. In my experience, everything is leading us somewhere fruitful. Even blind alleys and cul-de-sacs have a creative value. Those crumpled sheets of paper may have a few valuable pen scratchings on them that would give you some good ideas were you to revisit them in a calmer frame of mind. Maybe an idea would have the nerve to develop if you weren't shouting "Off with its head!" so early.

You complain of being blocked, but a block is really just the ego's resistance to working "badly." This is America, and we are very focused on product. We want final drafts, not rough drafts, and we want our perfection appreciated, dammit. As a result, we have one eye on our process and the other on its probable reception. When we ask "Is this any good?" instead of "Is this interesting to me?" we are asking the wrong question. What the hell, buster, work badly.

Do I hear you yelling "I can't, goddammit, and I don't want to! Why should I put bad art into the world?" We don't want

8

to just be artists. We want to be "good" artists—hence your wanting to dress the way you think "good" artists dress. (All right, all right. I admit there can be a certain comfort in feeling you look like you belong to a tribe.)

Let's get real. A great deal of bad art is already in the world. (Some of it made by very good artists in a choppy period.) If you are in a choppy period right now—and it sounds like you are—the best way out of it is more art. Art for the hell of it. Art for art's sake. A little bit of nonserious art for nobody's eyes but your own. Could you try it?

Making art takes guts. Choosing to be vulnerable and exposed rather than safely blocked is a risky venture. The ultimate reward, however, is truly great art.

Dear X,

My God, you've got a temper. I hope you're using some of that anger as fuel for art. You say that our correspondence is infuriating you. You are still fuming over my notion of something like daily productivity. Does that mean you might feel cornered into a little retaliatory art? I hope so.

Dear X,

You write that you are "not in the mood" to make art. What does mood have to do with it? And what is the "right" mood to make art? Any mood can be entered, just like a room, and we can make art from the precise place we find ourselves.

Anger fuels a lot of art—"I'll show them"—but so do joy, sorrow, tenderness, pity, even boredom. Take just one art form—music—and consider the many shades and nuances of mood that it evokes. Want exultant? Listen to Beethoven's Ninth Symphony. Need some clarity? Try Brahms, Johannes, Symphony no. 3. Want poignant? Try Mahler's Symphony no. 5, adagietto. Speaking of music, do you believe Mozart was "always in the mood"? Maybe he was, but for sex as much as for music. (He had to keep a roof over his and his evidently oversexed wife's head.)

Try this thought: maybe Mozart and Picasso produced as they did because they knew any mood was the right mood for art. Bored? Make art about it. Restless? Make art about it. Sad? Happy? Nervous? All of these moods make for art if the artist is willing. We think we have to "feel" inspired, but inspiration often comes once we have started and not before. I have a friend who carries a "doodle book," a small pocket-size sketchbook where she often catches large ideas, not small.

Creativity is like electricity. Throw the switch and it is there. But the switch is willingness, not mood. Believe me, Picasso was willing to make bad art—not, perhaps, that he often did. Dickens was willing to write bad prose. He wrote serializations and had to meet his press deadlines. Mozart, short of cash and on commission, dashed off a lot of his music. To my eye—and you will hate this—an artist is like a gadget, perhaps a word processor, in my case. The "art" moves through us. For years I kept a sign posted on my writing desk: OK, GOD. YOU TAKE CARE OF THE QUALITY. I WILL TAKE CARE OF THE QUANTITY. This wasn't to say that I didn't care about quality, but the "quality" is often better if I don't meddle with it too much—and my perfectionist, a.k.a. my censor, or inner critic, always wants to meddle. Give me something to write and I can always write it—unless I'm trying to write it well.

It's the "well" that freezes an artist up. It's the one eye on the review even as we are making something. Art is about process, not product. Picasso, Dickens, Mozart—do you think they gave a great deal of thought to being "great"? I don't think so. Picasso remarked, "We are all born children. The trick is remaining one." Children do not worry about masterpieces when they are playing. Of course, you may still be determined to make only masterpieces. Trust me—or don't—a lot of masterpieces were made in passing.

Dear X,

You persist in your petulant idea that I am urging you to make rotten art. I am urging you to make art, period. Some might be very good, some might be very bad. By making enough of it, regularly enough, you will improve your level of craft. I hope you aren't one of those artists who considers "craft" a dirty word.

Dear X,

Are you regretting this correspondence? Maybe so. You certainly took a huffy attitude toward my mention of "craft." I guess you are one of those people who think "art" and "craft" are two different things. You probably make a careful distinction between fine art and the other kind—whatever that is. For myself, I have never believed that making opera was more difficult than making a piece of finely blown glass, although one is "high" art and one is merely "decorative." Distinctions like this are lost on me. I find them counterproductive.

I am interested in making things, all sorts of things, high art, low art, in-between art. I like to make things, not so much take things apart. I like to create more than critique. Does this make me a philistine? It just could. You sound much more serious and high-minded than I do. You may exhaust yourself and your vitality by worrying too much if what you are making is "real" art or "serious" art. Just make it. To quote the great movie director Martin Ritt, "I don't have much respect for talent. It's what you do with it that counts."

I have a friend, a very fine writer, who says, "Fuck high art." And he makes some of it himself. What he is saying is that too much seriousness and cerebration sucks the juice out of an artist. To quote Martin Ritt again: "Cerebration is the enemy of art." He didn't mean that artists couldn't be smart, but that so often we use our fine minds to talk ourselves out of making art, or to pick it to pieces. (Perfectionists do not publish very much.) I think Ritt was an advocate of that Nike slogan, "Just do it."

"But do what?" you may yelp, still hoping to settle on the right masterpiece to rocket-launch your career.

Anything you do can be done artfully. Anything. Your current sculpture or painting. The soup you made for dinner. Your choice of kitchen-curtain material. Did I mention your hair? Hair really makes a creative statement. I know one writer who went through a shaved head phase, fairly shouting, "Watch out! Artist here!" and now prefers a careful, normal guy invisibility. "Average" hair. No statement. The fun of anonymity. You may think I am being facile, but what I am trying to say is that every choice is a creative choice, not just High Art. This makes all of life an art form and all of art a fine art.

So where does my mention of "craft" come in?

Making art is as natural as breathing. Just like breathing, you do need to do it, and with some coaching you can perhaps learn to do it better.

A singing teacher I know tells me that the first thing she always has to teach is how to breathe. Most people take shallow breaths and do not use their stomach muscles properly. A little training and they can sustain a much longer note. Well, it is the same with all artists. We may take to art naturally—like breathing—and need to make it, but that doesn't mean we couldn't still benefit from a few pointers. A young man I know just had his first singing lesson and he came away astounded by all he could suddenly do—just by breathing right. Now all he has to do is practice.

A little training—and a lot of practice—can help any artist. In my view, an art is both an art and a craft. Does that offend you?

Dear X,

You are right. I am "baiting" you a little. But you seem to like baiting me as well. Your most recent letter is a case in point. You are too busy to do any art, you report. You plan on getting back to it "when things settle down."

What makes you think things will settle down?

That's not my experience.

Artists have a lot of energy, and if that energy doesn't go into art, it will go into other things. All sorts of petty things will seem important—and you'll want to get them all "handled" before getting back to your art. People spend whole lives waiting to get back to their art.

A friend of mine talks about how minimal his worldly needs are. He doesn't need much money. He doesn't need much status. He can work at any menial job to get a little cash flow going for his low rent apartment. There is just one "inviolate" rule: early morning writing time—and his lovers have to respect this fact or they do not remain his lovers.

If you put making some art—even ten minutes of it—first, the other big and important things tend to fall into perspective. They suddenly do not seem quite as big or quite as important.

To be blunt, there is always time to make art. The rest of life is what takes getting back to.

Dear X,

I should have expected your latest volley, this one an attack of my evident lack of character. "Some things are more important than art," you lectured me—as if I had never loved my wife and my children or found a moment's time for them. (I did find time for them, but I found time for my art too.) In fact, it was when I had young children that I started getting up early to write. I still write early. (Not quite as early as my aforementioned friend who writes every day at four A.M. but early enough.) That gets it out of the way and then I am free to concentrate on the other very important things in my life. And I do have them.

Let me be blunt: unmade art is like a toothache. It's always there distracting you. You're always focused on that darn tooth. If you are writing a novel, the novel is always with you, always posing the question "What next?" Ditto for a sculpture or a painting in process. That brainchild wants your attention.

Unmade art will always pain and distract you—yes, even when you're supposed to be listening to your child's homework or focusing on world peace. Don't get me wrong or understand me too quickly. Children matter. They deserve to be really listened to, and we cannot do that if our unmade art is still competing for our attention. World peace matters, but you may not be able to do anything constructive about it today, while you *can* make art—and, in my opinion, if we put a little more energy into creation, we might put a little less into destruction.

Maybe all you can do about world peace today is make some art and improve your own goddamn mood. What do you think?

Dear X,

I'm delighted to hear that you are working. Not to be too smug, but it seems to have lightened you up considerably. I recognize that cheeriness may not be politically correct, and may even cause a certain amount of friction with some of your fashionably alienated friends, but it's still enjoyable, don't you think? I have always thought that the "press" on artists—broke, neurotic, lonely, sad, self-absorbed—applied more to blocked artists than to the functional kind. I have always found that a working artist can be pretty good company—not that it is chic to admit it!

You write that the more you write to me, the more dissatisfied you feel you are in your own life. Personally, I think it is the shift into actually making art that is changing you, your needs, and your wants. Art is an alchemical process. It transforms us just as much as it transforms the world. We cannot make art without changing ourselves. And some of what changes are our likes and our dislikes. Which means we yearn for different things in our environment. Our color sense may shift. We might suddenly want an orange wall or a neutral gray one. We may decide we need to live in yellow. Our environment becomes a piece of art, shifting shape as we do. We may suddenly start collecting things—or throwing things away. We may abruptly go for Zen serene or antique-shop clutter. The point is, our tastes will change—and we may need to change our externals to match our internal world.

On the other hand, and with me there almost always is an other hand . . .

It is interesting to me that suddenly your apartment is too small and you feel you cannot work full throttle without a studio. Are you sure? You may need "outer" space or you may just need some more inner expansion. Studios are expensive, and acquiring one might take all your available funds. It's up to you, of course, but sometimes we no sooner get started on a roll with our art—and it sounds like you have—than we acquire an expensive obsession that derails it. The obsession can be for or about anything—a new space, a new lover, a different and better day job that takes "just a little" more overtime to pay for the studio.

You see what I'm driving at, of course. But I just had another pertinent thought. Do you really need a studio, or do you just want one to look more like a real artist now that you're finally really making art? (You would be amazed at the shenanigans our ego can put us up to.) The acreage we require may actually be inner acreage. Your claustrophobia and feeling of being stifled may indicate a need for creative freedom, not studio space. A lot of art gets made in expensive lofts, but a lot of art doesn't get made there too. Sometimes an artist gets so worried about affording the new loft that he just stares paralyzed at its very chic walls. Think about it—and see if you can't do some work at your kitchen table.

Dear X,

I notice that your most recent letter was very chatty and filled with interesting thoughts. Not to discourage your correspondence with me, but don't you think some of your thoughts and theories should go into your work? (I can feel you boiling and feeling slapped down, even at a distance.) Stick with me a minute.

I don't always think our "artist" knows the difference between talking about work and actually doing it. It's not that our artist is "dumb," it's just that we should be using our materials to make art and not just talk about making art. This is why I trust the ditty: "The first rule of magic is containment/ the mastery of that allows entrainment . . ." Entrainment of what? Inspiration, of course. It can be encouraged, courted, wooed. You are, of course, already doing some of this if you write in a journal in the morning and take those solo expeditions out to explore our rich city. But one of the best ways to court inspiration is to practice a little secrecy. Don't open up your art to any and all comers. Don't give away the gold, as they say. Instead, make art your mistress and whisper a few sweet nothings—and that's *whisper*. To your art. Not to the whole wide world. You will find that a project can become far more stoked with energy if you keep it a bit more to yourself.

Speaking for myself, I am wary of what I call too much boast-and-toast talk. You know what I mean. Those conversations that begin with "That's very interesting, but what I am working on right now is . . ." I think it can take the wind out of your sails. It's like putting your project up for a vote depending on the reciprocity of your listener. A lack of enthusiasm can derail you. Too much enthusiasm can prematurely give you the reward for work well done. Remember that the part of you that creates needs to be shrewd about using its energy constructively. Too many bars are filled with too many wannabe artists talking about the work they are "going" to do. When?

In short, I am not sure our artist can tell the difference between talking about something vividly and doing it for real. I am wondering, for example, after that exciting night of "deep conversation and a few beers" you wrote me about—did you manage to get some work done? Just curious.

Remember that if you wake up "spent," that's a literal term.

Dear X,

Sorry you find me such a wet blanket lately. Frankly, I even found your description of that boozy evening exhausting. OK, I will grant you that I am an old and crotchety bastard—your mother might have told you that much—but I also like to keep my eye on the ball. If the name of the game is making art, making whoopee can be a dismal substitute, the creative equivalent of near beer. (You can drink it if you want, but it won't have much punch.) Talking about making art and actually making art are not the same thing. Have I now said that plainly enough? Let me give you a case history.

For three years a friend of mine tried to write a book. Figure out its structure, get a bead on its intended tone, shape it, train it, figure it out. He didn't write a word. Do I need to tell you he was miserable? And miserable to be around?

"Shut up," I finally told him. "Put it on the page." He thought I was a crotchety bastard too, but I found it painful listening to that book get pissed away.

"Look," I told him. "Pretend your book is one of those puzzles in a box. For three years you've tried to fit it together mentally without touching any actual puzzle pieces. Write the pieces down. Later you can scoot them around and see if you've got a mountain or a tree or a tiger."

"But—" he told me. (*But* is always followed by the excuse. The excuse is always disguised as a "reason.")

"Fight with me on the page," I interrupted him. Reluctantly, angrily, he began to write on the book instead of talk about the book. He began to lay some track. Pages began to mount up. He got excited. The last time I saw him, he looked years younger.

Art is actually pretty good for us, you see.

But enough about him. My point is that you and your young artist friends could all go out for "a couple or three" beers, talk about your "art" and how hard it is, and never get a goddamn thing accomplished. That would be tragic. (And it happens all the time.)

"But—"

But nothing. Write, paint, sculpt, compose—I don't care what medium you choose. Just stop talking about it and do it.

Dear X,

Thank you for your long letter in defense of the art of conversation. Did I say you couldn't talk at all? No, I believe I said to stop talking about your art. I believe I implied you could use the same time to make some of it. I can see why that made you angry—cornered into productivity again—but you could make some art about that anger too.

You used the word "fanatic" to describe me. You have built quite a case that I am an impossible and unrealistic taskmaster who just doesn't understand you and your many unique variables and pressures. Maybe I don't. In your initial letter you introduced yourself as a young artist. We seem to be getting an emphasis on the "young."

That bit about being too young to have much discipline— am I supposed to think your raging hormones have gotten in the way of your art? That would be a first. Hemingway made some art despite an evidently very active set of hormones. Channeled a little in the right direction, those same raging hormones provide good fuel for making art. Instead of having what you referred to as—I loved your phrase—"junk food relationships," try being a little more selective about where and how you spend your time. Try letting a little of your passion onto the page, the stage, the canvas. You might have a real love affair there. You could try it.

Dear X,

I am glad you got rid of those Plexiglas cubes. (I think they belong in fashion magazines with nude models draped across them.) But I am sorry you have concluded I am antisex.

I do not think I am "antisex." It is just that I know how closely intertwined sexual and creative energies are. I am not saying never get laid. What I am saying is be careful whom you get in bed with—in every sense of the word. Sometimes our romantic partners are bad for our art. They may encourage us to talk about it, not do it. No matter how adoring the eyes and how flattering the phrase, remember that "Tell me about your novel" is an invitation to not write it. Remember, too, that artists suffer less from too much outflow than from too much inflow. Our channels get clogged by too much small talk. Some lovers may simply talk too much for you to be able to hear yourself think. And art does take a certain amount of thinking.

On the other hand, if your partner sparks your thinking, that's wonderful. Some partners do double duty as "the muse," while other partners are suspicious of what they perceive as "this art stuff." They may dismiss your dreams of making art as "childish" and "not in reality." They may urge you to "consider the odds" and "be a little sensible." In short, they hope it's a phase you will grow out of. Frankly? I hope you don't.

Now, to continue on this love theme for a moment, lots of art has been made because of love—both unrequited and the other kind. We evidently owe the inspiration for *The Divine Comedy* to some woman named Beatrice. Robert Schumann married his muse, Clara, a pianist—who was the object of Brahms's unrequited love as well.

Any person who wakes us up is good for us. Any person who doesn't should be carefully avoided or seen in small doses—hard to do if you're living with them. In short, be protective and alert. You want to make love, but also make art.

Dear X,

You say my last letter gave you "food for thought." Let's look at that phrase a bit. It implies that thinking does require an inflow of nutrients, that some things will be fuel for our psyche and other things will be poison. In my experience, an artist requires a certain amount of structure—the staples of your diet—and a certain amount of adventure, the spice. Too stifling a routine and you'll grow fat and dull as if you're dining on institutional food. Too much spice and your artist won't be able to digest everything. It's a matter of balance, and everyone's recipe for balance is a little different—although, like the three squares, there are certain tried-and-true prescriptions for what a balanced diet is.

The mythology surrounding artists has us all dining on inspiration soup. Artists are portrayed as free spirits up at all hours of the night, wild and debauched, flaunting all convention. In other words, "artistic," a term I hate just as much as I hate the way we artists are typically portrayed. In my opinion, we have a lot of confusion in this country between alcoholism and "artistry." So many of our famous artists had a drinking problem—Hemingway, Fitzgerald, Pollock—that we think that art and alcohol go together like, well, scotch and soda. (We don't hear as much about the many artists who didn't drink or who drank moderately.) In Hemingway's case, we act like it was "art" and not alcoholic depression that helped him pull the trigger on that shotgun. Pollock died in a car crash, and we hear that as an artist's tragic death and not as drunk driving. The fact of the matter is that those men made art despite their drinking and not because of it. Your art is where the drama belongs, not your life.

As I've said, art takes a balanced regime: enough work time, play time, exercise time, and rest time. Also, for spice, that soupçon of adventure. We don't need adventure all the time, that's exhausting. But we do need it some of the time, say once a week, twice if you are working flat out. By adventure I mean some small solo expedition to explore something that intrigues you. Last week I poked into a great antique store and found a line drawing of a sailing ship that is right to order for the piece I am writing now. This week I explored an exhibit on Einstein. I particularly like his early letters to his wife. They were like, "Dear Kitten, I am playing around with some ideas . . ." Did you know Einstein said, "Imagination is more important than knowledge?" I'd say a little knowledge doesn't hurt either. A good adventure should awaken both.

Dear X,

You write that I am ruining your love life—by which I gather you mean your sex life. From the pitch of your letters, "junk food relationships," how much can love have to do with it? You talk about having great sex and rotten conversations. I think of great sex as a kind of conversation. There's a reason they call it "body talk." Of course, it takes the right partner, but I do think you might find that partner if you're a little more discerning. Good luck with your raging hormones—do I need to remind you that a lot of good art is about the need for real love and connection?

Dear X,

So you're working more. "To fill the empty hours," you say, now that you have severed several of your sex-as-snack partnerships. Good for you. But empty is what they were before. (Junk food contains what they call "empty calories.") Your letters sound a lot sharper now that you are on your own. I believe you're starting to see again. I think a bad relationship can be like a television habit—something that fills the hours but numbs you out a little bit.

You say you are "in withdrawal" from your lack of sex. Why not try thinking of it a little differently? Instead of thinking of it as "I gave up sex for a while"—like you might sugar, for example—think instead, "I am drawing my energies back into my own core for use along the lines of my own agendas."

You write me wondering how long you will have to be alone, and my answer is until you like your own company, until you can maintain your own company even in the presence of someone else. Autonomy is what you're after, the right to lively and independent thought. You don't want to merge and blur with your partner—or do you? You write that you miss having a warm body in your bed. What about your own? I hope your next partner is more than a warm body.

Dear X,

Please remember I am going only on the clues you give me. If you are not as shallow as you sometimes sound, make that clear to me. I would suggest making some articulate art about it. They call art "self-expression," but you have to have a self to express. Having a self takes some development—which, of course, is why they call it "self-development." You do have to do it yourself.

I'll tell you what I do for self-development—and it works. When I wake up, I do three pages of longhand writing just to see where I am and how I am and what I want to do with my day—which of course, more broadly, means my life. I suppose these pages are work, but they work for me and so I do them. I used to call them "brain drain" because they seemed to siphon off negativity. You might want to think of them simply as journaling, or even a "time out."

I do not have any way to prove to you that morning writing will work for you. You really have to try it. I find that for me, it prioritizes my day so that it tends to run along the lines I would wish for it. Perhaps because I am less absorbed by my own preoccupations, I am much more alert for tiny windows of time to be used for my own enjoyment. ("I'll just nip into that mystery bookstore for a second.") Instead of going through my day watching what I call the "inner movie," I am present and tuned in to what is happening around me. I see more than my own preoccupations and worries. On the subway I notice the old Jamaican lady with the crooked wig. I see the overwrought young mother, juggling kids and packages. I take in details so that later, when I need details, they will be there for me.

You know the expression "I was in a world of my own." When an artist gets stuck in their own world, work begins to become derivative. We draw on the "same old, same old." Our craft may serve us well in making something yet again out of the stocks that we have, but it is a little like making meals out of leftovers when what you need are some nice fresh ingredients.

The making of art is essentially an "image-using system." We reach into our inner well hoping to catch a little inspiration, a few images or ideas. If we have "overfished" that inner pool by not replenishing it with enough images, well then, when we go to make art, we may feel flat and uninspired.

Dear X,

You are working and I am glad to hear it. You are also now worried about whether your work is "original enough." I think this line of worry is a red herring—and yet I want to say that all artists have this worry sooner or later. We all want to make something "new" and "fresh"—as if the human condition doesn't repeat itself. But let's take a look at this originality question.

First of all, look at that term "original." The root word is "origin," and you are the origin of your art. If you are true to yourself, if you convey honestly and accurately what you wish to express, your work will be original. You may think I am playing with semantics, but I am not. When work is "boring"—which I understand to be your great fear—it is usually because it is not honest enough. There is a reason we speak of "the naked truth." (And there is a reason we all respond to nudity.) When a piece of work is nakedly and unapologetically itself, there is a purity, or, if you will, a nudity to it that commands our attention. It arouses our interest.

You write that you want your work to be "interesting." I can certainly sympathize, but again, that's a red herring. Your job is not to be interesting but to be interested. If you are interested enough by what is trying to come through you, you will forget your conventional self and respond in authentic and often surprising ways to the creative force moving through you. A friend of mine is a composer. He says that his work is "interesting" because he does odd things in trying to convey the precise tones moving through him. In other words, he listens to the demands of a piece of music and tries to find the sound that matches what he hears as the emotional truth. We all do this as artists. Writers do it with words. Painters do it with paint. Actors do it with gestures. We become a "hollow reed" filled with—and responding to—inspiration. When we respond with willingness and fluidity, "interesting" things happen in our art.

Creativity is not something you possess but something that expresses through you. You might call that something "inspiration." The point is, you need to step aside and allow this force to enter. Puccini claimed the ideas for *Madame Butterfly* were dictated to him by God. I myself have often sensed "higher forces" of inspiration. I sometimes think of ideas as coming from art itself. I went through a period of several years when I conceptualized this as "angels" of music, of painting, of theater, etc. In this sense, music itself wants some music written and we are merely the conduit. It certainly sucks the ego out of things, doesn't it?

Dear X,

It interests me that you don't believe in God, yet you still believe in creativity. For myself, I do not differentiate between God and creative energy. I do not picture God "out there." Instead, I tend to think we are all made of God making something more of itself. To put it differently, we are all creations of the Great Creator and we are intended to continue creativity ourselves.

Did you know Einstein called God "the Old One"? He was a highly spiritual man but not a religious one. At root, he believed that matter and energy were the same essence, that mass was made of energy. This has interesting implications for an artist. It posits a universe made of pure creative energy—which you may or may not call God. Everything is made from this energy, and that includes art. That makes God the Great Creator, or the great artist, whether you choose to believe it or not.

Because artists work from their inner core, many of us have experiences of inspiration, which I would define as conscious contact with the divine. I believe we achieve the same transcendent state making art that meditators achieve when they meditate. Time and space drop away. We are utterly absorbed by what we are making. Painter Robert Motherwell talks about the "brush taking the next stroke." When we are acting on inspiration, we lose our sense of ourselves as individuals. The art moves through us as our ego stands aside. For a writer, the word seems to find the next word. For an actor, the gesture seems to find the next gesture. This is why writers learn to "drop down the well" and let go. This is why actors learn to be in the moment. What is being in the moment but being in touch with God, who might also be called the Great Now?

Now, you are young and you have, one hopes, a long time to think about all of this. Better yet, you have time to experiment. Do not take my word for anything. Try letting a creative force work through you and see if you don't work more freely than when you consider yourself to be the "author" of your art.

It's just an idea.

Dear X,

I thought old folks were supposed to have closed minds. My "God" letter certainly set off a brush fire in you. You said I sounded like an evangelist. (Are all evangelists Bad? Can't they be carrying Good News and not just claptrap? I think they can.) Do my ideas threaten you? That certainly wasn't my agenda. In fact, I am not sure I have an agenda as relates to you. Agendas tend to drain the life out of relationships. So, no, I am not out to "convert" you. I am simply speaking from my own experience as, I recall, you asked me to do. I think you are a little touchy. Are you one of those people who believe that faith is for the intellectually impaired? Maybe you are.

To my eye, creativity itself is an act of faith. Every time we move onto the page, the stage, the canvas, we are committing an act of faith, and that takes daring. "I don't know what possessed me to try that," we say, and we are telling the truth. Something larger than ourselves—call it grace or inspiration— gave us the courage to become larger ourselves. Isn't that what we're all after?

A friend of mine has been working on an opera for seven years now. It is huge and unwieldy and glorious. He says, often, that he doesn't know what possessed him to make an opera. I think what possessed him was God or maybe the spirit of Opera itself. I think he is inspired, not just possessed, and I think artists are often inspired to undertake ventures that look patently foolish. Can you imagine the advice Wagner might have gotten about the Ring? I often think of artists as being a great deal like explorers. Did you know that when Magellan set out to sail around the world it was widely believed he would sail right off the edge? Did you know that there were supposed to be terrible sea monsters lurking off Africa? He chose to try his voyage anyhow on the grounds that the legends might not be true. That daring took an open mind, didn't it? An open mind leads to an open life, one with a flow of new and inventive ideas, ideal for the making of art.

Dear X,

You report now that you are working, but you are "bored." Who is bored? Which part of you? Not, I would bet, the part of you that is actually making things. The part of us that creates best is childlike. Have you ever watched a two-year-old explore a box of crayons? There is a whole world in that Crayola box: color, smell, taste, and a few other experiments too bizarre to mention. Are you approaching your art like that? Are you an explorer, or are you, prematurely, a critic?

It strikes me that your critic might be the one to come up with a word like "boring." (And your inner artist might agree just as a defense mechanism.) All of us contain an inner critic, a killjoy, censorious part that it is difficult, even impossible, to please. This is our adult, sensible side, and it can be death to creativity. To our adult—and dare I say calculating and even commercial—self, new directions had better look "promising," and what they promise had better be fame and fortune.

Our businesslike adult doesn't want us to "waste any time" by "just fooling around." It wants to know what the payoff is in dollars and cents. "This better be leading me somewhere," our adult side says, and if it doesn't, our friends will often say that for us. God forbid we take a detour just for the sake of it. God forbid we turn down a creative cul-de-sac. People, including ourselves, want our creative life to be linear, like a banker's career. I did A,B,C, and that got me to . . . But creative careers are not linear. Ask an artist how he got to where he is and he will talk about "lucky breaks" not "breaking in." He will mention "destiny" not "strategy."

We need to remind ourselves that a lot of great art doesn't seem like great art to the critical establishment. Van Gogh sold, what, one painting? He was supported by his generous brother Theo. Critics were not rushing to his door to hail the master. A great many masters and masterpieces are not hailed at all or are greeted with critical brickbats. Nijinsky's *The Rites of Spring* incited riots of protest. Hardly a promising reception.

Try to remember that the dead ends and cul-de-sacs that you explore may all be leading you somewhere—somewhere unknown. The unknown is never boring. Tell that to your critic and it just might back off. You may be less bored than "boring into something."

Good news about that kitten.

Dear X,

Of course I approve of your kitten. Anything with a little life in it is good for your artist.

We talk of "the play of ideas," and that phrase is telling. Children play and so should our artist. Great artists are often childlike. Despite being "serious" professionals, they remain amateurs at heart—from the Latin *amare,* "to love." It is a paradox of the creative life that serious art involves serious play. I think that kitten will help.

I once owned a little terrier who would present her ball and bark whenever my mood became too somber. I would be frowning over my typewriter, trying to will some "magic" forward and—"Yelp." There was the goddamn dog, right in the middle of my scene. I cannot tell you how I resented that dog's intrusions into what I thought of then as "my process"—and how right that dog was. I would stop to toss the infernal ball and right in the middle of "catch," I would catch an idea, the precise right idea to go on with my scene. Creativity experts will tell you that breakthroughs come as a result of concentration followed by release. We tend to want to binge on the concentration part. But it's the release that often gives us the "Ah-hah! That's it!"

Musicians may have the right idea. They "play" music. They "play" a gig. They "play" a piano. In other words, there is some alert, listening attention, some light receptivity in all of their expertise. Stephane Grapelli, the great violinist, once re-marked that "great improvisers are like priests. They are think-ing only of their God." I take that God to be the creative impulse yearning to whisper in their ear and come through in their playing. When we are too serious, we can miss the "still, small voice." It speaks as a whisper and not as a roar.

Why not see if you can keep an ear cocked toward what "wants" to be born?

Dear X,

You write that all my ideas about God and artists seem dubious. You are not "sure" about the "whole God idea." Did I ask you to be sure? How can you be sure without personal experience? I asked you to experiment. Do you have to be sure to try that? I'll tell you what I think. I think you want to "seem" sure. It's that matter of appearances again. Skepticism is chic at this point in our cultural evolution. Skepticism is intellectually modish. You don't want to "seem" gullible, you write. There's that word again, "seem." It tells me you're not looking at things for yourself. Instead, you are looking at "how do I look?"

Let's go back to that kitten. Doesn't it look foolish as it figures out the world? It tangles itself up. It tumbles. It reaches for things it can't quite reach and it takes a few falls. Yet, that kitten will figure out very well how to be a cat. "Cat" is its nature. I believe "artist" or "creative" is our very nature. I believe we, too, can learn to be what we are if we are willing to look foolish and take a few falls. There is safety in skepticism—but not much revelation. Bunkered in skepticism, hunkered down in "prove it to me," we try to put responsibility for our learning curve onto someone else—as you tried to do with me in your very first letter. You wanted me to give you answers, when what really serves you are questions.

"God" is a great question. You must find your answer to it for yourself.

Dear X,

I like the name Theo for that kitten. After Van Gogh's helpful, believing brother, you say. Good for you. I call that a vote of confidence in yourself as an artist. (If you had named that kitten Pablo, or even Vincent, I'd have taken that to mean you still thought someone else was the "real" artist beside yourself.) You write that Theo wears basic black and "looks" like an artist's cat. I've been holding out on you. I have a calico Persian myself. (I don't do dogs any longer for reasons I won't go into. Oh, all right. My legs are rickety and it's icy in the winter and I think I might fall and break a hip.) My cat is named Connie, after Constanze, Mozart's wife.

Here is what my little biography of Mozart says: "Constanze was not the perfect housewife. She spent money freely and loved to flirt. Nor did she fully understand she was married to a genius." It adds: "She did not inhibit Wolfgang, however, and shared a difficult life with him without too much quarreling, although she often adopted an independent attitude."

What a terrific description of a cat, don't you think? Connie likes to sit in the window amid my geraniums, watching the world go by. I like to sit in my reading chair, watching Connie. My walks are a little curtailed these days. I am waiting for a spring thaw to put "spring" back in my step.

Dear X,

You write that I mention walking as a habit. You're right about that. I hadn't broached it to you yet because we were still on basics. Now that you ask, I believe in walking daily. (And I do not believe in cell phones while you walk.) A good walk moves you out of the questions and into the answers. Einstein received the Nobel Prize for an idea he got walking home from his job at the patent office. Makes you want to try it, doesn't it?

Walking moves us out of our minds and into our bodies. We use phrases like "body of work" without realizing how literal the phrase is and that getting into our bodies might be one good way to accomplish that "body" of work. We also speak of a "body of knowledge." Our body does hold knowledge for us if we will listen. Therapists will tell you we carry memories of our past locked in our bodies. For this reason, a massage might make you weep as you "release" a memory. But the past is not all that is locked into our body. So is our future, and we can walk into it a step at a time. Walking, you will get what I call "alpha ideas," those ideas that point you toward your next work or breakthrough. "Why not paint about X?" you will suddenly think, and your work will head in a new and promising direction. (Or you can talk on your cell phone and keep yourself locked squarely in the present.)

I can see myself cutting short this discussion of walking because I cannot walk as I used to and that grieves me. I miss seeing a tree full of tiny birds. I miss seeing a fox dart into the underbrush. I miss the smooth slither of a garter snake slickly avoiding my footfall to quietly go his way. Walking in the city, I see Korean grocers with their festivals of color. Buckets filled with tulips and roses and daffodils, each in season. I love passing the low, flat racks of wildly colored fruits and vegetables. I love—hell, I loved it all. Maybe it is good that you write to me now that I am more housebound. Maybe I can take some vicarious thrill in your adventures.

Dear X,

I see that I've riled you up again. "Everyone uses a cell phone," you write—as if my mentioning it as a possible negative proved to you I was a doddering old fool.

Here's what I think: there's a reason we call it "small talk."

Not much conversation occurs on a cell phone, although a lot of "chat" does. You find such chat comforting, you say. Did we agree you should always be comfortable? I missed that part.

I once had the beginnings of a friendship with a nice young woman who one day told me that my questions to her made her feel "unsafe"—as if I were an incest perpetrator and not a mentor. I searched for words to reassure her, and then it occurred to me: growth is not supposed to feel "safe." When we feel a little "off center" and "out of the comfort zone" those are actually good things. Not comfortable, perhaps, but healthy. Sometimes, in order to hear ourselves think, we need a little silence. We need a little space to be with our own thoughts.

Art is an act of communication, and if we are constantly communicating our smallest thoughts, how will we have time for big ones? Cell phones miniaturize your life, breaking it down into tiny sound bites. I think we call them "bites" for a reason. They tend to devour our time and attention. There's no room for following your own train of thought. You can be interrupted at any moment—and you will be.

Virginia Woolf said writers needed a "room of their own."

Hearing that, I always think, "Fine. You build it. The rest of us can't always afford it." But what we can do is build a portable room of our own. My morning writing is the practice of solitude. So are my creative excursions and my walks. So is turning off the ringer on my phone during work hours. So is choosing not to have a cell phone. I have one young friend who carries a cell phone but claims that she "often" turns it off. I don't know that that is such a trustworthy plan. She is a young writer who is not writing right now. I think she talks her ideas away.

I believe we can all talk our ideas away. I think ideas form in our consciousness like stalactites and stalagmites form in a cave. If we interrupt the process to wipe away every drip, no large formations can be formed. Also, I believe we often turn to the comfort of conversation at the first sign of emotional or psychic discomfort. For an artist, discomfort may be like the grain of sand in an oyster—the necessary irritant that creates the pearl. So you see, I do have my reasons for encouraging you to autonomy and solitude. What you are after is independence of thought. Independence of thought may come only after a certain amount of discomfort. I may be saying "No risk, no reward," or even "No pain, no gain." The point is that I would like to see you experiment a little with just where discomfort leads you. Often it is the lever that switches us to a new and valuable train of thought. Experiment a bit and let me know what you find.

Dear X,

Enclosed, your most recent missive.

You can't win, can you? I received your long and chatty letter about your colorful walk through Chinatown. The lively crabs, the ducks hung in windows, the fish on ice, etc. I did not read it once I understood what you were up to. That letter was full of interesting ideas, and all of them belong in your art. Hence, I'm shooting the letter right back at you. Use it for more than talking to me.

Dear X,

Temper, temper. I seem to have hurt your feelings. What else would provoke you enough to call me "lonely" and "old" with "only a cat" for company? Save your pity and scorn for someone else. Connie is excellent company and so are my own thoughts. Not that you asked. Not that it occurred to you to ask. I am not in my dotage, twiddling my thumbs. Art is one of the few careers without a mandatory retirement age.

Even as we speak—or don't speak—I am happily at work on a new book. With my walking curtailed, I have had to find some housebound adventures for my mind, so I am learning Spanish. I love what my tapes sound like and now I am able to read a little of Neruda in his native tongue. I am also carefully tending a tank full of fantail goldfish. I got the fish for Connie. I call it "kitty TV," but I cannot tell you how much I enjoy the tank as well, how it sets my mind to swimming the depths.

In the old days, back when the snow was deeper and more frequent and we didn't have global warming to cope with, back before e-mail and television and radio, people had hobbies. They did needlepoint or played solitaire. These pursuits freed the mind to wander. They gave us mulling time, time to come to our own conclusions. The letter I returned to you was interesting, just a little wasteful. You had a whole set of fresh observations to use and you used them on me instead of on your art. It may seem that I am urging you to be antisocial. I am not. I am simply urging you to use more discretion about what I call "giving away the gold." Not that an old codger doesn't enjoy a long, chatty letter, but I am in a teacher's role with you and the lesson I am trying to teach you is to, in the old phrase, "hold your mud." Don't go sloshing your insides onto the outside. Let your art do that.

OK?

Dear X,

That was a long tantrum—or were you just keeping all your thoughts to yourself? I am glad you broke your radio silence. By now that kitten must be half cat. I took your silence to mean I had angered you, but now I see something much more serious was afoot. You weren't "in the mood" to work—and so you were avoiding me.

What makes you think you have to be "in the mood" to work? Some of my best work has been done when I wasn't "in the mood" to do it. Making art is like making love; one thing leads to another if you let it. The trick is "letting it." Sometimes we think we have to have an idea before we start. In my experience, starting begins the flow of ideas. It is as if we throw some master switch by our willingness to work. We put down a word or a brushstroke, and that action leads to the next action like a tiny chain reaction. The dominoes fall with just the lightest starting nudge from us. It is for this reason that I think of creativity as always present, a constant flow of spiritual energy we are able to tap into. I think of it as "dropping down the well" to a great underground river, a huge sea filled with usable ideas. You might want to try working from this universal source rather than from the battery of your own energies or ideas.

Did you know that Richard Rodgers sat down and wrote music from nine to nine-thirty every morning? Just like a banker or a factory worker, he kept regular work hours—and some of his most inspired melodies came to him during his half-hour routine.

I recognize that my attitude may siphon some of the mystery off making art. That's good. Most of the mystery around making art is a lot of hokum. Don't fall for it.

Dear X,

So you are teachable. I actually think artists thrive on a little structure, and I am encouraged that you took my suggestions to heart. I like your new schedule and I am happy with your report that you are once again productive. Notice how much less threatening I am when you have the self-respect that comes from doing your own work? I know that when we began this correspondence, you thought of me as a "magic teacher," that is, someone who could make you feel safe and secure while simultaneously coaching you along like Burgess Meredith did Rocky. Well, Rocky still had to put in the hours and so, of course, do you.

I'd like to say a word or two about having a "magic teacher." For the most part, I think such figures are a fantasy, a little like having a personal Obi-Wan Kenobi. On the other hand, humans do what they can for each other. Most of us can cite a teacher who made a difference. It's easy to believe that teacher was some kind of creative fairy godmother or Merlin figure, but the "magic" actually lies within you. You are the one who learns regular work hours. You are the one who taps into the creative flow or does not. The most brilliant screenwriting teacher cannot write your screenplay for you. Your painting instructor doesn't dip your brush into the paint. At best, a fine teacher is the floor sample for their own tool kit. They not only know how to use a creative hoe, they do use it.

I think it is important for you to realize that we are all in the same boat. Each of us, at any level of art, needs a good day's work. It's in doing the work that we gain self-respect. For some of us, that means getting up an hour or so before the rest of the family. For others, it may mean staying up later and learning to grab a nap. Many of us have day jobs, and day jobs have lunch hours that can be used to our advantage. A walk or a sketch can be sandwiched into a lunch hour. The year I was twenty-one, I carried a sketchbook with me everywhere. Waiting to meet my first literary agent, I drew the awkward outsize plant and stiff striped chair in his waiting room. A glance at that sketch, even years later, and I am right back in that moment, a young writer hoping for a break. The sketch, like a photograph but better because I made it by hand, freezes time for me. The Manhattan I saw that year is faithfully recorded. I still sometimes carry a sketchbook. Like so many writers, I still do an awful lot of waiting for things to happen. Most recently, I got my right shoe drawn while I was cooling my heels, waiting to see a publishing big shot.

Dear X,

I should have known you would be interested in big shots. Who Was It? you want to know, and What Happened? This goes along with your original theorem, why you singled me out for some mentoring: it's not what you know, it's who you know. Do I need to tell you I disagree? No single human power can ever make or break a career, no matter how much we yearn to believe it can.

If art is a spiritual activity and we are all equally sourced in God, then that tells you both what you need to know and who you need to know: God, in the form of creativity itself. Try trusting your unfolding to God and you will be just a little less shattered when a particular someone doesn't like your work. Believe that your gift comes from God and that using it is your gift back to God. Then you can see that it's what you know, not who you know—in the human sense—that counts. Of course, this is urging you to take a longer view of things than the notion of a sudden Big Break That Changes Everything.

But what about "networking" and "contacts," I can hear you yelp. I'd say that's putting the cart before the horse. Far too many young artists are busy trying to impress people rather than hunkering down to do the work that will, as a body, prove to be impressive. Do your work and then let that work do the work of attracting support. In the long run, it is the caliber of your work that convinces people to trust your artistry.

We are back to that question of appearances again. For a writer, having an agent is the symbol of being a real writer, but it is still the book itself that counts. A good agent cannot sell a bad book. (Although you might be cynical enough to think that a good agent can sell anything, I want to say that quality wins out.) A bad agent can sell a good one. Perhaps hype can win you one sale, but it cannot win you continued sales; it does not win you a career. Although our mythology would tell you a career is based on luck and who you know, both your luck *and* who you know will substantially improve if you rely on the Great Creator.

I don't ask you to believe my theory, but I do ask you to test it for yourself. Think of some form of support that you need for your art. Next, be alert for the synchronicity that delivers such help to your door. I use a very simple tool in order to galvanize such support from the Universe. Every so often, I simply make a list of twenty things I wish for. This list brings me clarity. Clarity seems to attract the next missing piece. I have a formula for this: clarity equals synchronicity equals manifestation. Experiment with this and let me know your results.

Dear X,

I'm glad I piqued your curiosity. I would like to give you an example of one answered prayer in your life. Your letters to me cited a feeling of loneliness, the need for another "warm body" in your bed. What happened next? You found that kitten right on your fire escape, yowling for help. You got company and a warm body to share your bed. The kitten's prayer for help also got answered. Have you heard the expression "God is efficient"?

Dear X,

Please remember that skepticism is a defense mechanism. You think finding that kitten was a coincidence. You do not see what your cat has to do with your art.

You can dismiss miracles as coincidence or you can begin to label coincidence as miracle. To me it boils down to this: expect to be supported and you will be. Support can come from any quarter at any time. Sometimes it's the timely hint that straightens out our technique. Sometimes it's the "break" that gives us encouragement when we need it. Support can come from your aunt Bernice or it can come in the form of a great new idea. The formula for support is ASK, BELIEVE, RECEIVE. Cultivate an attitude of expectancy, for it's expectancy that keeps us alert and optimistic. Attention and optimism are necessary to the long creative haul.

You may argue that you know some very pessimistic artists. Look a little closer. You may just be listening to the voice-over. It is chic to pose as cynical and skeptical, but any working artist has a working faith whether he conceptualizes it in those terms or not. Any piece of art is an act of faith. Do you think when Rothko began painting color fields he said, "This is going to really make my career"? No, he was simply following his nose, moving out of faith, doing the artistic "next right thing." Launching a new series of paintings takes faith.

So does the expectation that you will "somehow" find this

month's rent. Many artists display a great faith in what they might call providence. I don't think it matters what name we have for it, we all believe in Something, and if Einstein is right in saying that Something is made of pure creative energy, well then, that's a pretty good definition of God.

I think people often get hung up on a childhood concept of God. They were raised to believe that God was perhaps male, white, bearded, distant, punishing, withholding, judgmental, persnickety, and the lot. They have never closely examined their God concept to see what they are still believing in or have, perhaps, rejected. Their idea of God needs to be updated. They need to conceptualize God to be serviceable in their adult life as an artist.

For me, thinking of God as a form of spiritual electricity flowing where needed is a very useful jumping-off place, but there are so many things you may want God to be: playful, user-friendly, available, inspirational, supportive, solvent, and more. Clearly, the created world—as opposed to the man-made world we may live in—is filled with diversity and sheer creative glee. Remembering that, I always feel like I can count on divine help in my work. Essentially, I think of God as the Great Artist and I believe I will be sent what I need to make my art.

Such a reliance, while simple sounding, does get to the precise nub of what it is that I need to go forward: belief and support. If I can find that in God, I guess that makes me all the less vulnerable to human vagaries.

Dear X,

Your letter accuses me of having my head in the clouds or someplace else I won't mention. You don't want "support," you tell me. You want "money." I was already talking about money. Money is a concretized form of support.

When we talk about needing money, what we are usually after is access. We want money to rent equipment, for example, but what we really want is use of the equipment. We want money to buy CDs, but what we really want is to listen to music. Money buys that and guarantees us one form of access, but access comes in many forms. Once we begin looking for the universe to support our creative dreams, the universe is very inventive and even humorous in how it provides support.

Decide you need "more space" and get asked to house-sit a loft. Decide you need more or better supplies and land a day job at an art supply shop that gives a whopping employee discount. Decide you need more visibility as a writer and get asked to participate in an open mike. Sign up to participate in an open mike and learn about a newly started alternative press that is interested in having you submit to it. Opportunities abound. It is our openness to them that varies. Money comes in many forms, sometimes as barter. A month's dog walking may give you access to an avid editing bank. The walks themselves may give you a wonderful flow of new ideas. Ideas—do I need to remind you?—are yet another source of money. In fact, as artists, ideas are our major source of money.

You say that you are "broke," but to my eye you look independently wealthy. All artists are. We possess an inner storehouse that no one can take away from us. We have direct access to an inner river of creative energy that converts into money. True, you may need a day job, but no job is a dead-end job if it is a life-support system for our art. Then, too, there is the possibility that you could ask for guidance as to the "right" day job. When we ask for guidance, we are led, although our sign may not be a burning bush or the instant parting of the financial Red Sea. Sometimes, all we are shown is our next step. That next step is always the only step we need to take.

Dear X,

You write that you are "frozen in your tracks" and that you feel "fresh out of ideas." Let me give you a rule of thumb: you are never out of ideas; you may have too many but never too few. When you feel "stuck" it is because your ideas have created a mental logjam. You may feel like sitting in your studio and "figuring it all out," but don't do that. It's my experience you need a walk to get your energy moving again. That is what will pry loose one thought from the knot of thoughts and let you move forward.

Let me go back to a basic premise: creativity itself is constant; we are the variable. You may be overtired or discouraged, too tense or simply too busy, but the flow of ideas, insights, and inspiration is still right there for you to tap into. Although it feels the opposite, very often, when you are creatively blocked, it is from having too many and not too few ideas. You think, "I could try this or that or that or that . . ." And as the possibilities multiply, so do your feelings of paralysis. Have you ever seen a woodland stream blocked by too many sticks, leaves, and twigs? I have. And I have learned that if you jiggle a twig or two, perhaps pull a twig out, the whole blockage dissolves and is swept downstream. So it is with us. Try that walk, would you?

I have not asked you if you have continued with your morning writing. Many times, artists do morning writing until it "works" and then they stop. They go on their way, making art until they hit a snag and they again are blocked. I would recommend that you pick up the practice of morning writing again. Those pages keep the flow of ideas moving forward. They keep a gentle momentum going that nudges you into new territory.

Now, let's say you have kept up your morning writing and yet you still find yourself "blocked." I would ask if you have let your artist's adventures and excursions go by the board. Again, many artists use this tool only until it works. They go on excursions, encounter a new and enriching flow of insights and ideas, and then, when one idea seizes them with force, they focus on it and work it like they are mining gold and they'd better stay down in that mine. Do I need to tell you eventually they work the vein clean? If you have given up your excursions, start them again and do—am I beating a dead horse?—get out for some long, mulling walks. These will feel like "make work" until you have nudged your mind awake. Once that happens, your walks and your own mental processes will again be interesting.

Why don't you try these stratagems and make one additional rule for yourself: no serious work right now. Just fool around. We make a mistake bearing down on ourselves too hard when we feel ourselves to be stuck. What we seek is "the play of ideas" with "play" being the operative word. Don't hunker down. Don't pressure yourself to produce more work. Give yourself permission to lighten up. When we lighten up, we "light" up.

Do something silly if you are serious about moving ahead.

Dear X,

I am not surprised that your fooling around with a little "nonserious" art worked. I am also pleased that you have reinstated your tool kit. I consider morning writing, excursions, and walks to be like changing the oil and checking the fluid levels for a car—simply part of maintenance. Without them, is it any wonder that the engine knocks and seizes up?

Correct me if I'm wrong, but I thought I detected a faint disappointment that your convincing case of artist's block proved to be so fixable and predictable. Were you perhaps dreaming of five restful years on a psychoanalyst's couch?

I am friends with a writer who just went through precisely that. She had stopped writing and the "halt" solidified into a formidable-seeming block. She went to see a therapist who "specialized in creative people" and she spent several nonwriting years talking a good deal about her mother. At the end of that time, she understood a great deal more about her mother but nothing further about her writer's block. She was still just as blocked as ever.

It was at this point that she went to see a writer's block specialist. He was a very strict and serious guy—who hadn't written that much himself but knew a lot about theory. He encouraged her to dive straight into her most challenging work—for just twenty minutes a day.

"I felt like he was asking me to go off the high dive and I

was terrified," the writer told me. The invitation to the high dive didn't work. Too scared to put a toe in, even for a mere twenty minutes, the writer remained firmly blocked—which was her condition when I met her. I suggested that she try to lighten up.

What my friend needed to do was not "work" on her block but rather to "play around" with some ideas. Morning writing, excursions, and walks gave her a nonthreatening way to do that. Do I need to tell you she is writing again now?

Sometimes I conceptualize an artist's block as being like a large block of ice—attack it with a hammer and chisel and it just might shatter in all directions. Put a pan under it to catch the overflow and set it in the sun and the block will gently dissolve, leaving usable clarity. Usable clarity is what we are after.

Dear X,

You write that I take "all the mystery out of being an artist." By "mystery" do you mean "drama"? I think so.

You write that now that you are being so productive, you have "nothing to talk about." From this I presume you mean you no longer have anything to dramatize or complain about. Our drama is the hook we use to capture others' attention, often meaning "pity." Without it, we presume we are uninteresting, undeserving of affection and care. Put this way, you can see we have an awful lot besides mere art riding on our identity as a suffering artist.

Drama about our lack of productivity or money, about the "odds" stacked against us, has always yielded us a social persona. We've always had a way to say "But enough about you" and turn the conversational tide back to ourselves. Stripped of our wounds and war stories, many of us don't know quite how to relate. Being an "artist" gave us heroic stature, at least in our eyes and, often, in the eyes of our gullible fellows. Who are we if we are merely a worker among workers, a friend among friends?

We are a member of the human race. When we no longer try to stand above or apart from it, our art deepens. We move out from our limited perspective to a more humane and humanitarian one. If you are wondering where that is going to get you, the answer is very simple—to better art.

Dear X,

I am glad to hear that Theo is thriving. I take that to mean you may be thriving yourself, since you are bothering to notice—and take delight in—your cat. There's a lot to be learned from a cat, don't you think? My cat Connie can spend hours lying in a patch of sun—and yet strikes like a tiger when a fly buzzes past, too carelessly close. As artists, we are like cats: focused on the moment until an idea catches our attention and then we pounce. Like cats, too, we are both a part of and apart from our society. We are observers who hold their own counsel, particularly once we learn the art of containment.

What do I mean by containment? I mean the art of discernment practiced in all things. As we've discussed, we must learn to be discerning about our friends and our lovers. The Bard is right. Was it "much ado about nothing"? We must learn to marry well if we are to be merry. We must, however, also learn to be friendly to ourselves in our choice of friends. We must find our companions among the world's fuse lighters and booster rockets, not amid wet blankets.

As artists, we are resilient but also easily discouraged. As regards our ideas, plans, and projects, we must be very careful not to talk them away. You know that much already, but do you know how damaging mere indifference can be? Hostility we can counter with anger, making art "right at them." Indifference is a more subtle and insidious foe. It creates a breeding

70

ground for doubt: "Maybe it wasn't such a great idea after all. . . ." For an artist, the first doubt starts a vicious downward spiral—just like the first drink for an alcoholic. Indifference instigates doubt.

Does this mean we should never question ourselves? No, but it does mean we should not question ourselves mid-leap. We need to have confidence in our pounce to reach the other side. Agnes de Mille put it this way: "Living is a form of not being sure, not knowing what next or how. The moment you know how, you begin to die a little. The artist never entirely knows. We guess. We may be wrong, but we take leap after leap in the dark."

I like that image of artists as leaping. That has certainly been my own experience. I "pounce" on an idea, and though it may take me months or even years to implement it fully, I do not need or want to be questioned before I find my footing. I do not need to have someone say "You're writing about X? Now, why on earth would you be doing that?" The "why" is often as much a mystery to us as to other people. The answer may be as simple as "It interests me," and it should not have to be defended. I think it's almost always a lot of hokum when an artist can come up with a good intellectual justification for what they are doing, a *New York Times* Answer.

I can hear you thinking that one more time I am making artists out to be idiots. I know you want to think that art and intellect go hand in glove, and they sometimes can, I am sure—but not that often. Artists and intellectuals are not the same animal. One makes things and the other takes things apart. One creates and the other critiques. I am not saying that you need to sound stupid when questioned, but if I were you I would contrive to be questioned as seldom as possible lest someone pull the wings off what you are making. There is nothing sadder than a project that collapses in the middle, and I have found that if you examine the wreckage you can nearly always find some killjoy question that someone zinged right at the heart of a newly forming piece of art. De Mille is right, we take leap after leap in the dark and we use that dark as a cloak to protect our endeavors. If we take leap after leap in broad daylight, we risk having someone take a potshot at us just for the hell of it. I lost a whole novel to a potshot once. These days, I am pretty careful.

Dear X,

You write me that you want an "anchor in the sea of change." Well, don't we all? It would be wonderful if we had "security," but that is where faith comes back in. What I can tell you about your "sea of change" is that there is no avoiding it: change itself is the one permanent variable. Nothing and no one is static. We are all in the process of becoming something else—hopefully, more of ourselves.

You write that your lucky brother has a secure job—and he does, until he loses it. You yourself may have the most secure job. As an artist, your constant job is to respond to the ever-changing world. Perhaps you think I am being insensitive. Perhaps I am, but what I have found is that the dream of a constant world eludes me while the dream of a constantly changing world gives me an accommodating peace.

I can see that you are trying to lure me into a whole conversation about art and money, and I do not think that is a conversation we really need to have. My point is this: why wait to be paid to do something that you love? Make art for the love of it and money generally follows. Love money to the exclusion of your art and you will be both blocked and miserable. When I earn money at my art, which I often do these days, I think of myself as one lucky fellow, but I always aim to make art whether anyone is going to pay me to do it or not. This gives me a sense of largesse.

I think the artist leads the market no matter what the market tells us to the contrary. If we don't make it, "they" can't sell it. If I bear that in mind, I have some dignity. A little dignity is a nice thing to have, worth more, perhaps, than placing my "security" in the hands of an employer. You may think this sounds woo-woo, but I believe that as an artist I already have an Employer. I believe that God made me an artist and my making art is my way of saying thank you. When I am striving to do what to the best of my understanding is God's will, I believe I will be cared for. I think of the Great Creator as the Source behind all other apparent sources. I find this stance keeps me sane.

Dear X,

Try to have a little compassion for yourself, would you? You weren't brought this far just to be dropped on your head. God is the Great Creator. Phrased differently, God is the Great Artist, and artists love other artists. Whatever twists and turns your life takes, you will be carefully led and guided. You will be provided for. I can promise you that much. You are thinking about taking a day job, and you worry that this makes you somehow less of an artist. Worry if you want to, but the contrary may be true. Virginia Woolf ran a printing press. T. S. Eliot worked in a bank. Composer Charles Ives sold insurance. So did Raymond Chandler. A great many artists teach and in teaching, learn. In fact, learning may be the great benefit of day jobs. Art needs inflow and day jobs give us that. Day jobs bring us into contact with people, places, and things—i.e., raw material for making art. Not to mention, day jobs bring us both stability and structure. Did I say "money"?

I don't know where we got the idea that being a full-time artist meant no day job. Being an artist is a matter of consciousness. Having a day job doesn't alter that. I have seen more artists damaged by unlimited time than limited time. The year's sabbatical earmarked "Now write!" may actually be the greased slide to writer's block. No, I think we may do better burdened by day jobs so that we work to fit art into all available nooks and crannies. Better to always yearn for more time not less—as soon you will see.

You write that you are worried that a regular job may dampen your appetite for art. I think the odds are excellent that it may increase it. I remember vividly a year where I was carrying too heavy a teaching load—how I craved writing time! How I craved the chance to wallow in my words, mine alone, instead of shepherding the words of others. Finally, I got so pent up that I ran away from home to this fleabag hotel, where I holed up and started—you guessed it—writing. I wrote day in and day out. Deprived of writing for months, I now binged on it. I wrote the way a hoping-to-die alcoholic drinks, one shot right after another: chapter, chapter, chapter. I finished most of a novel in three weeks flat. Now, I don't recommend this form of working, but it did prove to me that my appetite for art had more than survived a temporary suppression. And so, about that day job dampening your creative appetite? Let's wait and see.

Dear X,

Do I get to say "I told you so"? I am delighted with your upsurge in productivity. That day job seems to be functioning as a booster rocket. You write that you are amazed by how much you can get done in the slivers of time available to you. What good news! Why is it so hard for us to realize that getting a great deal done boils down to getting a little done over and over again? You write me now that with small daily doses of work you are really laying track. That's really all it takes to make art, so why do we insist on making it so much more complicated?

A friend of mine has been blocked for several years by trying to write "the perfect book." The same few pages have been written and rewritten. Lately, the rewrites on those same few pages seem to be somehow watering them down. "What about rough drafts?" I finally caught myself snapping. "You're trying to write one perfect draft. So you write next to nothing. Try saying, 'This will take at least three drafts and then I'll see what happens.'" Freed to do rough drafts, freed to just "lay track," my friend is piling up pages again for the first time in a long time. "A little every day" is adding up.

Do I hear you say, "Of course it does"? I have been thinking. Maybe it is about time for you to find someone and start passing on what you know. Know any likely candidates? Artists have always apprenticed other artists. It's a good way to keep ourselves unblocked. The bromide is "You have to give it away to keep it." Have I had the grace to even mention how good writing to you has been for my own productivity? No. Probably not. Well, it has been. I think I owe you.

Dear X,

Why do you think I am opposed to your having "a romantic life"? My only caveat—albeit a big one—is that you manage an equal balance between "romantic" and "life." Your last encounter left you feeling depleted. Your lover dulled your appetite for life. Remember? You spoke of "too much togetherness" and a feeling that your personalities had somehow "merged and blended" rather than encountered each other. To my eye, you seemed to confuse "relation" and "ship." Your romance was a tiny canoe you climbed in together and neither of you knew how to paddle. As a result, you both drifted.

You write me now that you "don't want to drift into anything." My advice? Slow down. I spoke this week to a female recording artist, a singer-songwriter whose name you would recognize. She is reemerging into her life and her friendships after a year's stay in a boring and claustrophobic relationship.

"You know how it is," she told me. "After six months, the drug wears off." By "the drug," she meant "sex." She got into bed with someone she had nothing in common with except sex. "Then spent another six months pretending there was something more there that wasn't," she told me, laughing at herself. Meanwhile, no work.

Here's a thought. Find the "something more" first and then follow that up with sex. If this advice sounds archaic to you, it's because it is. It's the way it used to be done. An old man I know—even older than I—put it this way: "The trick is to find someone you like and then fall in love with them."

From my perspective, you already have a long-term, intimate relationship, and that is with your art. Your lover needs to love and accept this necessarily independent part of yourself. This means, of course, that you must love and accept it yourself.

Dear X,

Now you tell me. Sex was just a red herring. It's money you really worry about. "Either I can be an artist or I can be solvent," you write me. Where did this thinking come from?

I know we have a lot of faulty mythology about artists. We are described as flaky, irresponsible, drug-addled, promiscuous, and broke. I'm sure we can be all those things, but do we need to be? I don't think so.

What is it about working for love that makes you doubt such work will be valued? Look at how well you are paid for doing jobs you hate. Why not imagine you'll receive more for doing jobs you'll love?

"What are my odds," you write me, "of ever making it as an artist?" By "making it" you mean making money, and those odds immediately increase if you actually make art instead of just talking about it. What you don't make can't make you money, can it? I am thinking now about a friend of mine, a portrait artist. She suffered—and I do mean suffered—a nasty divorce three years ago. Her friends were full of good advice, most of it boiling down to "get a job." She told me, "I already have a job. I am a painter. Can't they see that?" What her friends saw was that she had been left with a mortgage to pay, and they thought she might have a better chance of paying it with a job, say, at the local florist. My friend hung tough. She chose to believe she would be able to make it banking on her talent. It's been three years now, and to date my friend has been proven right: her job was to paint. (Which isn't to say that for some of us a day job, especially the right day job, isn't a fine idea.)

Dear X,

You write me a little crossly that I seem naive. The odds, as you explain to me as if I'm learning impaired, are stacked against you. Let me be blunt. I think "the odds" are a drink of emotional poison. No one invokes "the odds" who isn't trying to keep you from committing creativity. For one thing, your odds of succeeding immediately increase if you try succeeding. Your odds of publishing a novel, for just one example, are a lot higher if you write a novel. You may think I'm being facile, but I think I am simply responding to spiritual law: "God helps those who help themselves." "Ask and you shall receive," even, "Knock and it shall be opened to you."

When we believe "the odds" are stacked against us, we are choosing to believe that "the odds" are more powerful not only than our own gifts but also than God. If the tiny mustard seed can become a tree, if the acorn can become the oak, why can't our ideas flourish into mighty manifestations? It comes down to the question of self-worth, doesn't it? We tend to believe we must "deserve" good fortune, but what proof do we have for that notion? Did the lilies of the field earn their place in the sun? No, it was God's good nature to care for them, and it is likewise God's good nature to care for us and our brainchildren. When we see our work as an extension of God's work and not as an act of ego, it is easier to believe that there may be a plan of goodness for it. If we believe "Not I but the father doeth the works," then we really do not need to worry about the question of odds, do we?

At root, "the odds" are an argument aimed at leveraging us back into being sensible, but what proof have we that it is the true nature of life to be sensible? Are zebras sensible? Are puffer fish? What about baboons, sea anemones, calla lilies? To my eye, we have very little proof that the Great Creator is, or ever was, sensible. What are the odds involved in making snowflakes? Odds simply do not factor into tiger lilies, tulips, or daffodils, do they? Or think of boxers, collies, Weimaraners, fox terriers, Scotties, beagles, rottweilers, Westies, and cocker spaniels. Someone was having an awfully good time with diversity. What are the odds of an English bulldog? A bloodhound, a borzoi? No, odds do not seem to factor highly in the Great Creator's creations. Why should they matter much to us?

Dear X,

You didn't like what you refer to as my "dissertation on dogs." You are talking about "business odds," you tell me. Why do we consider "business" more intricate and complicated than the business of life itself? It seems to me that the minute you make "business" outside the realm of God's scope, you are setting up a case for false gods, as in "Thou shalt not have false gods before me."

I can almost hear you rattling your modernist sword at me and accusing me of being "biblical" rather than pragmatic, but is it a question of "rather than"? What if the whole world, including what you think of as "business," does turn on a spiritual axis? What if a healthy spiritual life equals healthy business as well? I was interested to read an interview with Steven Spielberg, who has done quite well for himself on a business level. He related a fantasy that when he arrived at heaven's gate, God would say, "Steven, thanks for listening."

Certainly many business tycoons speak of following their "hunch" or their "intuition." What is that, really, but a more secular way of talking about the "still, small voice"? From my perspective, our business lives begin to grow more sound as we place our dependency on an undergirding of spirit. Perhaps an active spiritual life is actually good business practice. Perhaps a grounding in faith gives us the courage to either "risk" or "hold fast," as seems indicated. What is it about faith that seems so foolhardy to you? Or is it simply that faith does not seem chic?

Dear X,

You write that I treat you like "a total philistine." You are not an atheist, you say. Since you are not a believer and you are not an atheist, I believe that leaves you an "agnostic," that is, someone who just doesn't know. To my eye, this is a useful jumping-off place and, if you are willing, I think you could try an experiment in open-mindedness.

To begin with, try a week of media deprivation. Don't read. Don't watch TV. Don't listen to talk radio. Stop doing life "as told to you by" and try listening for your own thoughts and perceptions. Experiment with solitude and with a few healthy walks. Get out on an excursion or two and see if you can decide for yourself the kind of world we live in. Most especially, I want to recommend walking.

I believe we automatically stretch our minds and perceptions as we stretch our legs. Take a look around you. Watch people interact. You may find there is as much or more kindness afoot as cruelty. Simply consider the evening news and the negative spin it puts on our collective experience. We do not hear the broadcaster announce, "Thousands of beloved grandmothers made it safely home tonight." Instead, the "news" is the one old lady who met with violence. Our news breeds fear. It breeds a sense of the world as an adversarial place. But is the world so adversarial? This is something for you to decide. Today, on my way home from a newsstand, I saw the bottom

drop out of a little old granny's paper bag. She clearly felt help-
less and hapless, but a half dozen people rushed to help her.
Someone snagged a spare bag for her from the newsstand, and
she was sent back on her way with an onrush of goodwill. I
think this sort of small, good-natured scenario happens all
the time.

Experiment a little with being open-minded. You may find
yourself openhearted as well.

Dear X,

You remark that you do not see any connection between an "open heart" and making art. I take this to mean that you see art making as an intellectual pursuit. Are you certain about that? Consider the word "heart" itself. Doesn't it contain the word "art" as well as the word "ear"? What is the act of art making other than the act of listening to what would be born through us? Doubtless, you think I am merely being clever, but I am actually reporting my experience. When I am working at my best and most free, I experience a sort of hollowness—as if I am a space that is filled by inspiration rather than a person seeking to be inspired.

We think we must "be inspired" to create art and that this inspiration must have an emotional force to it. That is not my experience. I have done some of my best work from what was essentially a neutral position, not unlike a court stenographer. When I was striving to "get something down" rather than to "think something up," I seemed to be onto something. I think this is where the notion of service can enter. We can make art in the service of something, and that spirit of service gives us a workable humility that allows us to hear our cues. There is a listening receptivity that allows us to make art as a non-premeditated response. Another way to put it might be to say that art is less about throwing the ball than it is about catching the ball. Life tosses us the ball. We catch it and toss it back. We are receptive and responsive. We are in the moment—but it's all pretty casual.

If you think of the artist as being like an oyster, if you think of life as the irritant that causes the pearl to form, you begin to see art making as a natural, even automatic response of our human nature to experience. Thought is what you think about life, while art is what you do about it. When we think of art making too cerebrally, it smacks of theory and of therapy. It becomes a reaction rather than an action, and art is too primal for that.

How is your cat?

Dear X,

Of course I think about your cat. I think about you and you live with a cat—and happily, it sounds like.

I think you are onto something with your cat habitat. Watch your Theo as he moves from level to level. All those different perches and perspectives must be very enjoyable: I think you can take a lesson from that, trying to go through life as an alert observer, looking at things first one way and then another. This is why I am such an advocate of walks. It is excellent to alter our routes through life. It changes our thinking, refreshes our perspectives. Why, just this week I remembered that if I cut west one block earlier than usual, I am on a street of great old brownstones. The window boxes are things of glory—geraniums, petunias, trailing vines with the occasional cat basking in the sun on the sill. I wished Connie the cat could be out with me, getting an eyeful of her confreres as they bask in the sun. Have you noticed how your cat alternates rest with intense attention? This is what I am advocating for you with the intense focus of morning writing followed by the release of an adventure or excursion. (You can think of that excursion as hopping from perch to perch.) I want you to have a cat's agility at capturing the full glee of the moment. And, yes, I did say glee.

People talk a lot about the peace that is to be found by living in the now, but they seldom talk about the untrammeled joy that can be found there as well. I went, last night, to a small Oriental restaurant for dinner. I had my usual, the $4.95 cold sesame noodles special, and I had a wonderful half hour's meditation staring at the giant tank of carp goldfish—one black one, two spotted ones, the rest gold—that they keep right by their doorway for good feng shui. I cannot tell you how those fish both calmed and excited me. I wasn't really thinking about working, but when I got home, I found I had a "buzz" of sheer good feelings and so I spent an hour or so just putting it onto the page. My Chapter Five has a little extra zest to it now.

Dear X,

I received your disheartening letter conveying the fact that your family was urging you again to "be sensible." I have never understood what was "sensible" about trying to ignore the things you love. What is it about being a declared artist that people find so threatening? I don't know. In any case, I am sorry for the pressure you are under and I suggest you repeat to yourself the following: "If I give in, I will only feel more pressured, not less."

Ours is such a pedestrian culture. We have no place in it for the "calling" to make art. Perhaps if we talked of art more as a form of invention and entrepreneurship, we would have more enthusiasm for it as an American enterprise. In America, we respect ambition, but somehow an ambition to succeed in the arts strikes "sensible" folks as harebrained and illusory. I don't think it is. There is honor to following your vocation (from the Latin *vocare,* "to call"). Beyond honor, there is also the matter of success. I think of that as "filling the form," as in "If the shoe fits, wear it." In other words, if you are called to be an artist, you may just be *supposed* to be one. And who is to say you will not be a successful one, even in worldly terms?

I sometimes wonder what would happen if we were to corner one of our know-it-all relatives into talking about their own lives for a moment. Are they truly happy? Do they have a sense of job-well-done at each day's end? Do they feel that the paycheck is the only thing that they like about their job and do they feel that that is enough for them and should be enough for us? I do not think, for myself, that the money can be the only measure of success, although in America we are certainly cued to think of it as the foremost. I think there is something to be said for feeling that we are in our proper role, that the shoe fits, as I said before, and that we can walk in our shoes without them pinching. I am friends with a writer, an estimable writer, who for eleven years cleaned houses and washed dishes to support his writing habit. That's a lot of dishes and a lot of dusting. But it was also many years when he went to the page a happy man. I will tell you something else about this man. He is comfortable in his own skin. He seems to be aging well, with a sense that his life has been well spent. That happiness and sense of right action must count for something.

Dear X,

You write me you are "discouraged." Further, and worse, I gather you are disappointed in yourself that you have such feelings. You feel you shouldn't. You say such feelings make you doubt that you are "really" an artist at all. This pisses me off. I think the press has sold us a bill of goods. We are taught that there is a mysterious and elite tribe of "real artists" who never get discouraged. Hooey.

I have never met a real artist who hasn't gone through discouraging times, sometimes discouraging years. Art is a calling, a spiritual calling, and like any other vocation it is subject to the dark night of the soul. Doubt is simply part of the spiritual domain. All artists are beset by doubt, some sooner, some later. Doubt doesn't mean we are doing anything wrong. To the contrary, doubt may mean we are doing something right. I think of artists as being like trapeze acrobats: we leap and hope to catch the bar on the other side. We may doubt, but we set aside our doubt to leap. I have a friend who is an estimable equestrian. She tells me that in the formidable grand prix classes, where the jumps are very high, a rider must "throw his heart over the fence and jump after it." Artists do this as a matter of course.

Take a look for a moment at that word you use, "discouragement." *Coeur* is the French word for "heart." When we are dis-couraged, we are moving away from our heart and what it loves and knows. When we are en-couraged, we are trusting our heart and what it urges us to. I have a technique I use when I am discouraged. I set up a dialogue and give my heart a chance to speak to my mind. It goes like this:

HEART

I am so sad. I feel hopeless.

MIND

What do you need from me?

HEART

I need gentleness right now and I need to rest. I don't need
you pushing me all the time.

MIND

But if I don't push—

HEART

I know a thing or two about rhythm, don't you think?

MIND

I guess you do. You lead us for a while.

HEART

That's better!

I can hear you thinking, "Oh, dear God, what a codger. He
is just full of these little bromides." Well, try it, why don't you?
Experiment a little. I have survived a long time as an artist and
I have survived, in part, because I have been willing to find the
solutions instead of just the problems.

Dear X,

You are full of surprises. I am glad you tried my little "trick" about a heart dialogue. I am glad you learned you are too hard on yourself and that art might arise from you naturally if you just give it a chance.

Yesterday I baked all day. I was quite a sight—flour all over me, head to foot, and where there wasn't flour there was confectioner's sugar. A friend came by last night, surveyed me and my baking extravaganza, and said, "Here's where all the creative energy went today."

Hearing that, I thought, "What a healthy attitude." My friend saw creativity in my cooking and not just in my cooking up some idea. Are you able to give yourself credit for creative living? I hope so. Maybe my next mail from you will be a tin full of cookies. (Your mother's oatmeal raisin are my favorite.) I can dream.

Dear X,

Your mother's fudge recipe was delicious—and so was your insight that you could trust yourself to go back to work after making some. Chekhov advised actors, "If you want to work on your art, work on yourself." Henry Miller advised young artists to fall in love with the world. Since candy is a symbol of love, I'd say you're doing pretty well with both Chekhov and Miller. I've never believed an artist's life needed to be one of either abstemious deprivation or depraved indulgence—balance is what you are after, and a little sweetness is good for that.

I have a friend whom I am worried about lately. He is, in his words, a hardworking artist—a concert violinist of the very first water. He tours internationally and teaches on a prestigious faculty. But he is so mean to himself. He flogs himself forward through teaching and rehearsals. He is tired much of the time, but he never turns his phone off and simply allows nature to take its course restoring his "ravell'd sleeve of care"— or his bow arm. Although he is still a young man, I am worried that he is burning himself out.

There is a direct relationship between self-nurturing and our capacity for a sustained creative flow. We don't want to work spasmodically and sporadically. We want to work consistently and creatively. This means we must treat ourselves as finely tuned mechanisms. We must learn what makes us thrive and give ourselves a diet of those nutrients. Enough soup. Enough sleep. Enough exercise. Enough diversion. Enough companionship. Enough enough. And so, thank you. Your fudge helped me to thrive. I enjoyed a very good day's work.

Dear X,

You write that you are growing impatient for your "big break." To my eye there are two dangers in that concept: "big" and "break." A career is not made by something large and sudden. It is made by many small daily actions adding up. This "adding up" may take the form of sudden recognition, but the work itself has nothing sudden about it. Even "sudden breakthroughs" require the years of work leading up to them. And look at that other word, "break." You don't really want a "break," do you? You do not want your life and your personality to shatter under the impact of new visibility and velocity. Again, the very word "break" carries a warning with it. People, just like things, do break, and the onslaught of attention, opportunity, and opportunism is enough to break many of us. There is a saying in 12-step programs, "Pray for a slow recovery." For artists, the thought might be "Pray for a slow success."

Notice I am not saying "no success." I am saying pray for a success you can handle. A "big break" can lead to a "big break." I'd like to see you survive success and even thrive in it.

Do you read the tabloids? I do. I think they are full of excellent cautionary tales. We learn a great deal about the human capacity for folly when fame and fortune come too quickly into a life. I am thinking now of an excellent young actor, one who had no sooner nipped his drinking problem than he acquired a gambling addiction. He has just changed horses and is still racing down the track to self-destruction. The tabloids are full of stories like his. To read them, you might think the rich and famous are all fools—or you might think, as I do, "Ah, success is truly that hard to handle."

Dear X,

You are too harsh. "Why," you write me, "must the voice of experience always be so negative?" I am sorry it sounds that way to you. You write you find me "antisuccess." I don't consider that fair. What I am opposed to is the kind of success that is its own undoing. A friend of mine, a successful man who has had his turn in the barrel of sudden success, calls success "the unseen enemy." He points out that our mythology tells us that success ends stress, where reality teaches that success engenders a different form of stress.

Now that we have something to lose, we become afraid of losing it. Some of us do lose it—the cash and prizes—because we suddenly overdo it to medicate our new anxiety. We spend money we don't have—or that we're going to have only once. We overdrink, overdrug, oversex ourselves because success can make us so numb with terror, it takes a cattle prod to wake us up. We don't set out to be self-destructive, but we become that way. The wheel spins faster, and so do we. The tabloids are actually excellent cautionary reading for the price tag on "big breaks." You see, they do break some people—and very nice ones.

Dear X,

I didn't mean to take the wind out of your sails. Of course I hope you "make it," but more important I hope you enjoy making art. If you enjoy the process of art enough, it will give you a measure of safety against fame, which is a dangerous by-product, not an end in itself. If you like making art, the question of making it as an artist tends to fall by the wayside. When you are focused on what you are doing rather than how you are doing, you can have some very good times.

There's a lot to be said for making art. In the actual moment of making it, you are never old. In that actual moment of making it, you are never poor. Art is made by tapping an inner resource that flows outward. In this sense, it is like spending. You are operating from a sense of spiritual generosity. Because of this, in the actual moment of making art, no one can make you feel less-than. When you are focused on your own learning curve, you experience your own burgeoning sense of beauty and competency. Competition falls away. So do the worries of the world. In fact, involve yourself deeply enough in art and the world becomes a viable place. You cannot encounter your art except in the exact now. This is what spiritual seekers of all stripes are after: an experience of the power of the now. (God has been called "the great now.") As an artist, you must focus on the now, meaning on God, although you may never conceptualize it that way. You experience "art" as a form of the verb "to be." This experience of living in the now is the experience all spiritual seekers lust after. It is the "big thirst" that Rumi talks about. We experience it routinely, lucky us.

This morning, I woke up early. The sky to the east was rose gray. The buildings below my window had a soft glow. I took to the page. I am working on Chapter Five of a new book right now and Chapter Five of a new book is working on me. I meet my work with a certain daily eagerness. I feel less that I invent my work and more that I encounter it. I do not know what I will find each day, but I do know I will meet something that is waiting to meet me. In this sense, work is my great love affair. I sit down at my desk the way I imagine a Parisienne lover might slip off to a rendezvous, with a frisson of the erotic always present. I have never understood when people make work out to be a drudgery. That is so far from my own experience and, I hope, from yours. The time when I am working is like a time apart from time. Do you experience work that way? It is like a heightened moment of awareness, the kind that people do yoga asanas in order to encounter—and the encounter is made for us simply by "showing up." Are you showing up for your work these days? Do you show up with all of you present? If you do, you will be so richly rewarded.

Dear X,

It's good news about your walking more. (I can also understand your resistance to it. Your mother, after all, was a great walker too, and who wants to be like their mother?) I have to say, I already sense an optimism in your letters. Isn't it interesting how nothing can change, yet everything does? That is the power of our attitude. This, again, is where I feel our animal companions are so good for us. They model the notion that all of life is interesting. Today my cat Connie decided that a dead spider was a wonderful toy. She got a good half hour out of moving it here and there, scooting it along a window ledge. Finally, I had to see what it was she found so fascinating. The answer: a dead bug. I do think a cat is the perfect prototype for an artist. It takes so little to capture its attention and so much can be made from the slightest thing. In this sense, I think life rewards the attention we give to it. If we treat life as if it were fascinating, it tends to be.

You write to me about your brother with his good "secure" job and his emphasis on new gadgets. He wishes he were writing a novel, but instead he is watching his new DVD player. I think when we have an authentic yearning to make something, we can buy it off only so many times. Our inner artist knows that DVD player is no real substitute for trying a novel. I agree it's tricky breaking that news to your brother. He may need to buy a few more gadgets before he'll believe you.

I am thinking again about my friend the dishwashing writer. He has a very solvent brother as well. For years he tells me—the years before his work "suddenly" took off—he was considered the family black sheep. No one could fathom what he was doing at a poverty-level job—even if he insisted his life was brimming with inner riches. Now, on his last book, he finally got what might be called "a good sale." Just like that his black-sheep status shifted—and it disappeared altogether when he got a movie sale. It seems that no matter what he says to his family about the joys of work for work's sake, what they really understand is cash on the barrelhead. Sounds like he should meet your brother, doesn't it? Maybe a few words from someone outside the family loop could win you a little peace. Oh, I doubt it.

Dear X,

What a bothersome day I had today. I was scheduled to do an interview and all the questions were about the perceived "difficulty" of a life in the arts. I wanted to say that a life without the arts is what strikes me as difficult.

"It must take such discipline," one comment ran, "to work every day." I said, "Discipline? What it really takes is simple curiosity. I want to discover what I am thinking and feeling, and work is how I do that."

The interviewer was not to be deterred. "Isn't it terrible, the tendency in our schools to de-emphasize our creativity? Shouldn't we do something about that?" the next question ran. Again, I found myself saying so much of what I say to you, "Just make art. Just make an artful life. Let the other chips fall where they may." I guess I would rather be pro-art than anti-academia. I believe we have a great deal of freedom and that we can choose to use it or ignore it. If we are focused on what the academics don't do, we may lose our sense of what it is we ourselves can do.

"It must be so demanding, living off your own inner resources," the interviewer continued. I felt like saying, "Now, wait a minute. In the larger sense, don't we all?" but there was no point in getting into it. I wasn't going to convert that interviewer into a believer, and that interviewer, hopefully, was not going to convert me. He was a pessimist disguised as a realist, and I am an optimist disguised, at least to my eye, as a realist. It's a great deal like the question of love. Either we can worry about being loved "enough" or we can focus on being more loving. Only one of those choices will make us happy.

Dear X,

Your new friend sounds interesting—and interested in you. I like the questions about your work and the understanding that you might require time and space to do it. For the first time, it seems you have met someone who is saying "Tell me who you are," rather than "Be what I think I need."

Your reticence about sex does not strike me as an ominous sign—although it clearly does you. No, it seems to me you are weighing the variables of what you stand to gain and what you stand to lose. On the gain side, there's yet another notch on the gun, so to speak. (You have not lacked for partners, just partnership.) On the loss side, there is your fear that physical intimacy might cost you psychological intimacy. It can do that, so what do you have to lose by slowing down? Allow the base of friendship between you to strengthen. You may find that as you do so, your sexual attraction will increase, not wane. It's worth trying, I think.

Quite apart from your pending relationship, you write me that your time is broken up and you get no long, uninterrupted swathes for working. My advice? Pretend that you will never have such time again. Tell yourself that all of your days will be as crowded and as pell-mell as those you have had lately and then figure out how to work in them. Unlimited time is like an unlimited bank account—not a luxury most of us will ever get to enjoy. You have heard the bromide "If you want something done, ask someone busy to do it." That holds water. Limited time can increase our focus, making us make the most of the time that we have got.

To my eye, an artist never has enough time, and so it is up to us to make time. We need to safeguard our time against other people and their however-well-meaning agendas for us. One way I make time for myself is by taking the daily time to write each morning. It is paradox. The pages take time but they give me time. They prioritize my day so that I do not misspend it along others' agendas for me. Another thing morning writing does is to miniaturize the censor. I write and my censor, an inner critic, shrieks, "You're so grumpy, so petty, so negative, so vague, so something that I hate. . . ." I hear that censor, but I keep right on writing. There is no "wrong" way to do morning writing—it's free-form. Because there is no wrong way to do it, over time my censor learns to stand aside. This is a portable tool. My censor is trainable. This means that when I have time, I can use it. The censor can start up, but I don't need to take it seriously. I can dive past it straight into work. This means I do not need huge amounts of time to work. I can work in whatever time I've got available. In my experience, there is both never enough time and just enough time, barely. I believe morning writing is what makes the difference. What do you think?

Dear X,

If it's not one thing, it's another. You really keep me hopping with this mentoring business. It seems the minute I put out one fire, another one flares up. Your fires are always breaking out on some new front. Take the current drama. Aside from your new and hopefully significant other, who appears to be both good for you and good to you, it sounds like you've fallen in with some lower companions. You write that you have been involved in a number of "heady" conversations about the state of the arts. I don't see that talking about the state of the arts is going to help you get much art done, but that may be the precise point. A lot of people who are blocked prefer to think the world is blocked. That certainly lets them off the hook, doesn't it?

You write that you miss the "stimulation" of the old days of argument and discussion. Well, since you used the word "stimulation," I'll use the word "masturbation." So much boast-and-toast talk has a masturbatory narcissism to it. It seems to me that a lot of very good work gets done without a lot of talking about it. You can be sure that as you sit in some bar, jabbering about how hard it is to work, someone else will be home quietly working—and that person will eventually get ahead. You talk about "making the scene," and I think that is a very different skill and agenda from making the art. You may believe that if you seem like a "hot" artist, you will magically be a "hot" artist, but a great deal of the hottest art actually gets made by those who are cool enough to skip the public auditions you seem to be getting into.

Remember that art is about being interested, not about seeming interesting. You would be amazed by how much serious work goes on right under the radar. I think of artists as being a little like moles—and not so much like peacocks. The mole is always secretly, productively tunneling away, making quiet little inroads and pathways. If we are always focusing on how unappreciated we are, then we don't need to focus on whether we are being appreciative, do we? Life will need to be loud and public to get our attention. It will require volume just to get past our own mental PR, the "you're so great" voice-over we are listening to. And volume is deadening. We will need the voltage of a mental cattle prod just to feel anything at all. It's like sex toys. If sex is fun enough without them, you don't need them, do you? So, for me, it all comes back to what are you really doing? What art are you actually making? What is delighting you recently? What subtle thing has caught your attention and held it? As I wrote you, my cat recently appreciated the hell out of a dead spider. What do you appreciate lately?

Dear X,

I am not urging you to be "antisocial." I am urging you to be selective in your companions. Companions require care and upkeep. Some relationships pay this back and some do not. It's your half hour. How you spend it is up to you. You can spend it decrying the state of the world or you can spend it actually experiencing the state of the world. I am all for adventures, and the more subtle and daily they are, the better. Get to know your neighborhood. Do that and your neighbor's adventure becomes your own. Notice the new pot of geraniums set in the widow's window. Maybe she is again entertaining callers. Maybe her life has turned a corner for the better and you are a witness. It is very rewarding to be a witness. In fact, I would say that it is one of art's primary roles, don't you think? It was Ezra Pound who remarked that artists are "the antennae of the race." I believe he was talking about our responsiveness, the fact that we are always paying witness.

You write that your "friend," whom you are slowly getting to know, is full of interesting questions. Bravo. I think questions keep us alive as much as answers do.

And so, a few questions. What are you doing these days to explore beyond your comfort zone? Are you doing any interesting reading? Have you been to a good show or movie? Whose thinking sparks your own? I have recently been reading a superb novelist named Tim Farrington. One way or another his books are all about God, or our relationship to God and our consequent relationship to the afterlife. As you know, these are among my favorite subjects, and so I find his thinking challenges and expands my own. I do believe that we encounter the consciousness of an artist through his or her work. Sometimes some of my liveliest relationships are with people whom I may never meet at all except on the page.

Dear X,

Your point about Jane Austen is very well taken. A life does not need to be lived broadly to be lived deeply, does it? You seem to be living more and more deeply right where you are. This pleases me no end. It is exciting to me that your walks seem to be strengthening your connection to the world. It is astonishing what a shift a small change in pace can make, isn't it? You write that as you "slow down," faces seem "luminous with humanity." What a beautiful and accurate phrase.

It interests me that you have had a shift in thought concerning your desire to be "original." At the start, you longed to be "original," meaning, it seemed to me, "different." Now you write you are more interested by being "authentic." In the long haul, this may make your work more original. Ironic, isn't it? As you come to an increased interest and respect for others, you desire to make art reflecting this interest and respect. Inherently, such art will have dignity and a sense of focus. We will trust that you know whereof you speak. This is all good news.

There is a very real sense in which an artist is a reporter and a reporter is a witness. We trust a witness who speaks accurately of the facts within his observation. As an artist, it often seems to me that you are charged with the same thing. You not only say "It looks like this to me," you also include enough details of your own thinking that we know why. I guess what I am driving at here is the need for two things: authenticity and specificity. If either of those is missing, we do not trust the artist's voice.

All too often, we put the cart before the horse. We talk about the need for an "original voice" without talking about the need for that voice to have something to say. If you have something you feel deeply about, something that truly issues from your soul, then you will have the "voice" to say it with. "Voice" follows from and doesn't precede self-expression. So what does your self wish to express?

Dear X,

You write me that you want a life beyond your art. Have I ever seemed opposed to this? I get the impression you think my life has nothing in it but capital A, Art. No. I have friends, family, the aforementioned cat. I have obligations to community and to ongoing creative projects. I have letters to write, calls to return, errands to run. In short, I have quite enough life to not get much art done in it. This is why I defend art making. There are days I am lucky to get in fifteen minutes, but I make sure I do, at least, get in that. In fact, I have a fifteen-minute rule that every day, day in and day out, no matter how much or how little time I have, I must put fifteen minutes' time into my art. With luck, that fifteen minutes becomes elastic and stretches into more, but at least it never shrinks. I won't allow it.

Here is what I have found. There are a number of days when fifteen minutes of art is all I get done. There are a number of days when I get more done. Because there are no days when I get less done, I can fairly say I work at my art daily and that daily adds up. It is remarkable how much we can get done once we get rid of the fantasy of time. We will never have unlimited time in which to make art. Our time will always be limited and sometimes severely; by accepting that unpleasant given, we get a great deal accomplished.

The year that I wrote my best-selling book, I was teaching

full-time on two separate faculties and I was deeply involved with my family. My daughter was having a "bumpy" year, and that took a lot of time and attention to try to straighten out. In order to write my book, I set aside fifteen minutes a day, hoped to stretch it to forty-five, and aimed at the rough draft of one short chapter per week. Instead of making my work fragmented, this system seemed to make it cohesive. I probably wrote better in that period than I have in many others, and it was all because I resolved to use well the little time I had.

Dear X,

I can see I've made you angry again. You think that I make a life in the arts sound too much like a life on the assembly line. You don't want to punch a clock, you say. You don't just want to show up for work, you write to me that you want to make "good" art. Who can blame you? The only problem with making good art is that sometimes in order to make good art we have to be willing to make bad art. Styles mature spasmodically. Sometimes we write poorly on our way to writing better. Sometimes we paint poorly—on our way to painting better. When we demand that we always paint or write or draw well, then we are putting our critic in charge of our creative process. And we deny ourselves the dignity of growth. I keep a sign posted in my work area that reads "I am willing to make bad art."

Sometimes visitors read that sign and are appalled at me. I have to parse it out for them. The sign does *not* say "I plan to make bad art." It merely says I am willing to make bad art. By being willing to make bad art, I am free to make any art—and often that art is very good. Just not "perfect," as the critic in us would like. Make no mistake, the critic is a perfectionist.

The perfectionist cannot stand the messy process of making art. The perfectionist prefers the finished-product stage. The work is "done" and that work is "good." When we listen to our perfectionist, we stall in our tracks. This afternoon, I had a visit from a filmmaker. Ten years ago, he made a promising first film and for ten years now he has been expanding that small film into a feature. Why has this expansion taken ten years? Because it's really a contraction. Instead of working from his artist, he is working from his perfectionist. His perfectionist has him rewriting the same twenty-five pages over and over.

"You have no idea the weight it would lift off me if only I could finish," the filmmaker tells me. But I do know the weight. We have all felt the crushing pressure of perfectionism.

"Put up a sign in your workplace, 'I am willing to write badly.' Read that sign daily and let yourself work," I told the filmmaker. "You're not operating out of your artist anymore. You are operating out of your critic. Give your critic a nickname and send him out of the house. Say, 'Good-bye, Timer. I'll speak to you later.'"

I am hoping that a few more artists will name their critics Timer. (So named because the perfectionist always has a pedal to the metal about perfection.) It could become a turn of phrase: "Stop Timering me about it" or "Don't be such a Timer."

Meanwhile, don't be such a Timer. Of course you want to make good art. Just give yourself permission to make bad art in the meanwhile.

Dear X,

Sometimes you really delight me. I am so happy to meet your inner-critic Timer. I am so happy you dropped the rock about good art and let yourself make some art, period. Am I wrong, or did I detect a little telltale enthusiasm, the veiled hint that you just might be onto something. In short, it sounded like you were having fun. I think that's the best kept secret of all: it is fun to make art.

Dear X,

You write you are worried that the holidays will disrupt your schedule. First things first: let's celebrate that you have a schedule! I cannot tell you the pleasure I've gained this year watching as you got your feet underneath you. It's a paradox to me. We start off worried that we will "lack the discipline" to do morning writing. We find soon enough that morning writing does not *take* discipline but it does *make* discipline. What is it about stumbling blindly to the page, not knowing what we think or feel, that does tell us, later in the day, just what it is we must do to feel better? As I recall, my writing this morning was about my lack of sleep and general lethargy. Lo and behold, I worked two separate sessions on two separate projects today. It just "occurred" to me that it would feel good to work—which it did. Without morning writing, I doubt I would have heard my "cues."

Have I mentioned to you my more than half-serious idea that artists should take a note from Alcoholics Anonymous? In AA, it is one alcoholic talking to another that makes it possible to go a day without drinking. In my ideal scenario, one artist talking to another becomes the support necessary to go another day creating art. I believe there is a magic in artist-to-artist contact. It keeps our eye on the ball.

Just as an alcoholic who doesn't drink has had a successful day in the big picture, so, too, an artist who makes art has had a successful day in the big picture. Just as it is emotionally sober to not drink and destroy ourselves, it is emotionally sober to make art—and something more of ourselves.

Believe it or not, there is a 12-step program for recovering artists called Arts Anonymous. They have a concept—correct, I think—that artists derive an anorectic high from not making art. We become addicted to the avoidance of our art. As with any other addiction, lies, half-truths, and evasions help us to protect our habit. Another similarity is the lapse of self-responsibility and the tendency to blame someone else. It becomes our family's fault or our lover's fault that we are not making art. The bottom line, of course, is that it is our own fault. We are the ones who avoided our art for a day. The person, place, or thing that was the "reason" was really just the excuse. We all have lots of good excuses for avoiding our art, just no good reason.

At the other extreme is what I call the "art bender." That is when we want to binge on our art, using it to block life instead of to live it. Today I talked to a newly recovering writer. For a decade, he has struggled with a block and now, gently yet miraculously, he has undertaken his morning writing and started writing. What he wants to know is this: since it feels so great to be making art, can't he please, please binge on it?

The answer is no.

If we are after a long-term life in the arts, that life must be built on sobriety and not on bingeing. Binges bring hangovers. Hangovers bring the inability to work. What we're after is the gentle succession of successful days building one at a time upon each other. Learning sober work habits means learning to live such homely slogans as "one day at a time," "easy does it," and "first things first."

A sober work life may lack the wildness of a binge, but it also lacks the remorse of a hangover. Yet, just as it may take another alcoholic to really understand the demoralization of a drinking bout, so, too, it may take another artist to help us remember the "esteemability" of a good day's work. I know that in writing to you, I have been grateful for my own long-established work habits and I have been so happy to see those habits taking root in your life as well.

Dear X,

First, you write me worrying that holidays will disrupt your work schedule. Next, you're worrying that your work schedule has disrupted the holidays. I think it is wonderful you are concerned with the impact of your work on others. Still, it strikes me that your overall equanimity hinges upon your working—no matter what others think.

Let me one more time draw what may be an unwelcome analogy. When an alcoholic is drinking, everything else is up for grabs. Nothing matters more than the drink, and "nothing" means "no one." Let us say this alcoholic now gets sober and worries that by not drinking he will make others feel bad. Perhaps he would, but not as bad as his drinking might make them feel. Now turn the focus back into making art.

For quite a while you have been learning how to make art quietly and gently, how to have a life and make a life in the arts. The drama around your productivity has calmed way down. You can no longer complain of being blocked because you're not. In a slow, quiet, positive way you are productive. Now, you wonder, should you give that up because it might make people feel bad? The answer seems obvious. And so, X, why not do the obvious? Keep gently working.

Dear X,

I am sorry you consider me, one more time, a fanatic. Perhaps I am. The idea doesn't really bother me very much. "Keep gently working," you quote back at me as though I have asked you to fly to the moon. All I have really asked you to do is stay steady as she goes. I admit that can be hard but not as hard as the alternative. I remember too clearly the days in which I was not working. My "not working" had a way of dominating my days that my "working" cannot begin to emulate. "Not working," I was always obsessed by "working." "Working," I am free to be interested in the rest of life.

Still, I recognize that I may have made making art sound like washing windows—you just do it and try to keep your balance in the process. Perhaps it doesn't occur to me that I strip away the glamour because what is left is still so interesting. A life in the arts is a long Socratic conversation—question after question arises and is answered by art. "What do you think of that?" I ask myself, "that" ranging from politics to pumpkin pie. There is nothing too large or too small to be considered.

It is perhaps this habit of questioning that sets the artist's life apart. Unlike a banker's life, or a doctor's, or a teacher's, an artist's life is not about how things have been done but more about the question of how things could be done. An artist paints, dances, draws, writes, designs, or acts at the expanding edge of consciousness. We press into the unknown rather than the known. This makes life lovely and lively.

I think of artists as cartographers. We map the world as we find it, rather like Lewis and Clark did, sending back sketches of a continent emerging from beneath their fingertips.

Dear X,

In answer to your question, I do not believe all artists are identical, but we may be very similar. I tell you stories about my artist friends and you apply them to yourself. You ask me about some problem that seems yours alone and I reply with some story about another artist friend. Yes, we're all in this together, I think.

First of all, I think all artists are both easily encouraged and easily discouraged. Knowing this, we can be vigilant. We can be alert to when we are disheartened. We can be careful to keep ourselves well championed. This is why morning writing, the primary tool of a creative life, is a daily tool. We need a daily tool because damage can happen daily, almost in passing. The ability to spot the damage and circumvent it is a learned skill.

A friend of mine just wrote a small novel. That novel went out to five readers. Three liked it very much. One hated it. One didn't get around to reading it. That made three positive votes and two negative ones. My friend took the negative feedback from the one reader who didn't like the book and ran that feedback past the three who had liked it. The consensus was that the negative response was just "off." My writer friend went on to another draft.

Why am I telling you this story? Ten years before, the same

writer gave an early draft of a book to only two readers. One responded positively, the other responded negatively. Fragile and low in self-worth, the writer allowed the negative vote to carry the day. He put the embryonic novel in a lower desk drawer, where it lived out the rest of its days. Should he have known better? Maybe. Should he have been stronger? Maybe. The point is that he wasn't, and many of us are not. We artists are what creativity expert Natalie Goldberg calls "delicate." This doesn't mean we aren't good, but it does mean that we can be all too easily thrown. We need stratagems to keep us from getting thrown. For writers, multiple readers whose aesthetics we know and trust are one such stratagem.

For all artists, before, during, and after friends are another key stratagem. These friendships keep our artistic endeavors within the larger realm of an ongoing friendship. Within that context, we can report in when we are in a hard patch. We might ask for and accept help to support finishing a novel or a series of paintings just like we might ask for some help on running the homestretch of a marathon: "Just stand there and cheer for me, would you?" Like runners who need supporters at the the twenty-second mile, we need to learn to make the phone call that says "Pray for me. I need a little inspiration." Our art must not be so rarified and so special that it falls beyond the reach of our friends.

Of course, you may feel I am one more time deglamorizing art. Perhaps I am. I guess I believe art has enough inherent glamour not to need much enhancement. What I am saying probably boils down to this: the best reason for making art is the sheer love of art. Once love is involved, how much mysterious hokum is really necessary? The beloved is already endlessly interesting. So you see, I think art can withstand a good dose of the ordinary. I'd like to see art become a little more like bowling, something anyone can try even if a strike takes some doing.

Dear X,

I am very interested by your acquisition of a new friend, an "art buddy." If you have chosen well, this addition to your life should prove invaluable. What you call an "art buddy," I call a "believing mirror." No matter what you call it, its importance is immeasurable. An art buddy is someone who mirrors back to me my competency and possibility. Rather than bring up the odds against me, an art buddy reflects the odds in my favor. I am a winner, not a loser. I am a taker of good risks, not a gambler. An art buddy sees my potential to win out, not lose out. An art buddy helps me to believe in myself.

Your letter asks why it has taken you so long to find positive support. My theory is simple: positive support is unfamiliar. Many of us grow up not with art buddies but with "fun house" mirrors. Our desire to make art is reflected back to us in a distorted form, not as normal and natural but as an act of the ego. "Who do you think you are?" fun house mirrors ask us. "Aren't you getting just a bit big for your britches?"

"Who do you think you might be?" art buddies inquire. For those of us who grew up in the fun house, an art buddy can be a radical departure. Even to our own eye, we look good—can that possibly be OK?

Ours is a culture that describes artists in very negative and inaccurate terms. We are flaky, irresponsible, broke, drunk, drug addled, promiscuous. An art buddy tells us otherwise. Is it any wonder it's hard to believe?

Dear X,

You write you are worried about "losing yourself in your art." I'd be more worried about finding myself there. Every time you make a piece of art, you locate yourself, your precise position, on the longitude and latitude of your experience. You learn who you are and what you believe. Right now you are writing a play. Doesn't that commitment make it totally clear that the Bard was right and all the world is a stage? Don't you overhear scraps of dialogue, stumble happily across pieces of plot? Of course you do. Once you have declared yourself to be making something, you encounter a collaborative synchronicity all about you. You don't need to be "obsessed" about your art. The universe seems to do that for you. Clues and great ideas are everywhere. Your job is to be alert and open to the cues as they come up. And they do come up.

"Here is how it looks from here," art says. The artist reveals the art; the art reveals the artist. If you are worried you will become overly immersed in your art, there, too, you will meet yourself and you have already built in some safeguards against self-absorption. Morning writing puts your "inner movie" onto the page. Creative excursions and weekly walks involve you with the outer world. Your recently acquired day job is another safety net. And so, it could be argued, is art itself.

As I've remarked, Ezra Pound called artists "the antennae of the race." This phrase captures something of the artist's outreaching curiosity. The artist both reflects on the world and interacts with that world. The world flows both to and through an artist. As artists, we "take things in," not just take ourselves seriously. Art that takes itself too seriously loses the "play of ideas." When we lose that, we're dead in the water.

I think we have been working together long enough now that you have some inner sense of when you are in a good phase and when not. You have begun to do some very necessary and healthy self-policing. I have kept up this habit of self-scrutiny for years. It serves me. I have remarked to you before that I think the artist's way is a spiritual path and that like most spiritual paths it must contain a necessary element of self-inventory. I am not talking here about neurotic self-involvement and narcissism, but I am talking about an ingrained habit of self-assessment. We are the ones who must ask Am I being honest? Am I being open? Am I still willing to express what it is I see? To be an artist, you must deliberately cultivate a beginner's mind.

Dear X,

Now you write that you are impatient. Who isn't? We'd all like to be "further along than we are." *Commit* yourself further and then let me know how it goes. It is a rule of thumb that whenever we feel the universe has let us down by not delivering the goodies soon enough, there is some small step that we are trying to evade taking. Take your next step and see if the universe doesn't take one to match it.

Dear X,

It's going well, you write me. Now your question is "Where?" But a career in the arts is not linear. You do not get to point Z by going A, B, C, D, E, F, G . . . As artists, we may never get to point Z. There will always be some place hovering on the horizon that we haven't gotten to yet. And so, when we ask "Where am I going?" the only real answer must be "further." The interesting question is not "Where am I going?" but "How am I doing?" And we must mean to ourselves, in our own eyes.

A career in the arts is not like a legal career, a business career, or an academic one. We do not progress neatly, year in and year out, taking a proscribed series of jumps, making a trackable record of advancement. We hope to get "better," of course, but there may be no proof for years at a time and then, suddenly, we may zoom ahead—not necessarily in our skills but in the level of attention they attract. As I have warned you before, most "overnight" successes have been working far longer than overnight. The book that is singled out for sudden praise may not be the "best" book. The painting that wins the award may not be our favorite or the one most interesting to us personally. Sudden "breakthroughs" are all too often exactly that: the shattering of the known career. This is why the question "How am I doing?" must always be answered in personal terms and never in terms of "How do I seem to be doing?"

The surface of a creative career may not convey its depths. We may seem to be moving smoothly from accomplishment to accomplishment when this growth is actually accompanied by inner turmoil. We may seem stymied exactly as we are grappling most deeply with questions of longstanding interest to us. For this reason, the question "Did I work today?" is always the real question. If we are working, then "things"—meaning a career—will somehow work out.

Let me tell you a story. Early in my career, I saw myself as stalled. I "worked" daily but I saw that work as going nowhere. I was frustrated and I was scared. What if I never had a breakthrough? What if my career went nowhere? What about "me"? Was I a fool to stake everything on art? Then I got an irate phone call from my agent. A network executive had called him with a work assignment for me. And how, exactly, had my work gotten to the network executive? my agent wanted to know. I had no answer. The answer seemed to be in the work itself. Someone had seen something and passed that something on to some someone. . . . It was never clear, but what was clear was this: I was clearly the ideal candidate for the project the executive had in mind. In one fell swoop my career went from "nowhere" to "somewhere." I was not only caught up to where I thought I should be, I felt a little beyond my depth, in over my head—and days before, I'd worried over being left behind.

"Not everybody has a deus ex machina," I can hear you scolding me, but what makes you so sure? We use the word "creator" to denote God, and isn't "creator" another word for "artist"? Perhaps the Great Creator does take an interest in our careers. Perhaps his eye is not only on the sparrow but also upon us. It is possible.

Dear X,

You write me scornfully that my cheery little stories are just that—stories. You can believe stories are "just" stories or you can believe, as I do, that stories are an oral tradition passed from artist to artist, generation to generation. There is something irrefutably valuable in the experience, strength, and hope of someone who has been where you are trying to go. This is why I value artists' autobiographies. I've been warned they are self-serving, but I've seldom found them that way. Artists tend to be truthful where art is concerned. I am thinking now of a favorite book of mine, *Musical Stages* by Richard Rodgers. From this book we learn that although he fought both depression and cancer, Rodgers strove to write daily, every morning. Not working, he was miserable. Working, he was less miserable. For him work was not only the answer but the only question worth asking. He loved his work and left us a legacy of nine hundred-plus songs to prove it.

You can read other books on Rodgers and learn of his alcoholism or his womanizing, but it is his positive addiction to work that interests me. It is in his commitment to work that he shares his experience, strength, and hope with us. Work brought out the best in the man. Work, given a chance, brings out the best in most of us. There were many days when Rodgers was not inspired but worked anyway—many of his most "inspired" melodies came from those flat days. Do you think there's a lesson here?

Dear X,

You're in love and you're working. Now you want to know "Is this normal?" Why does this remind me of a Polaroid sent to the Playboy Advisor? If I were in love and working, I don't think I'd be looking a gift horse in the mouth. But, to answer your question, art is not made from only pain and negative emotions, it is also made from love. As I remarked to you, *The Divine Comedy* was crafted out of love for Beatrice. That's a lot of poetry and, perhaps, a lot of love. I am not sure where we got the idea that love and art could not coexist, for they can. Your letter is merely the newest, latest proof. Have I said I am happy for you? I am.

Dear X,

No, I do not think it is compulsive to set goals. I do it every New Year and several times midyear as well. The trick, I think, is to set goals that are reachable—and in alignment with your true values. I also like to work backward. If I want something completed in one year, what must then be done by nine months, six months, three months, one month, one week, today? I also try to set goals in more than my work arena. I try to acknowledge that there is more to my life than me and High Art.

To do this, I use another tool, Setting the Compass True North. Numbering from one to twenty, I "wish" on the page. Those wishes head me True North. Those wishes convert to goals through appropriate actions. For example, "I wish I could play the piano" becomes one lesson weekly and one half hour of practice daily. I "wish" I had a richer spiritual life becomes explore churches on Sunday, explore classes on Wednesday. And so forth.

In making my goals list, I try not to overwhelm myself. I keep my bedrock tools in place—morning writing, creative excursions, weekly walk—and then I block in my work time and, after that, I add in the new. In this way, I keep unfolding "on track."

There is one trick to setting goals, I think. And that is to always leave enough breathing room for the divine to enter. We may have a goal, but the Great Creator may have a different and even better goal that has not occurred to us. It is for this reason that I try to invite the participation of the Great Creator when I make my lists. "This or something better," I always note at list's end. You might want to try it.

Dear X,

Friendships can endure through thick and thin, but there are also times when we reluctantly must let a friendship go. From the tune of your last letter, you've reached that point with your troublesome friend. (Was he one of your boast-and-toast colleagues from earlier? I would guess yes.) The question to ask is this one: am I being a friend to myself to continue in this friendship? The answer, alas, sounds like no. You write that your friend is overly dramatic, always staging dramas on your deadlines. I call such a friend a "crazymaker," and most of us, when we start out, have lives that are filled with them.

They distract us from making our art—and from the art we are not making. As threatening as life with a crazymaker may sound, it is often less threatening than a life where we ask ourselves to be consistently creative. Once we do that, crazymakers are out the window. This is the turning point you are now at. Your choice is between function and dysfunction. I am confident you will choose well.

Dear X,

You are not the "hole in the doughnut." You just feel that way. Make no mistake, it is threatening to give up friends and habits that no longer serve us. We feel like we are leaping into the void. "Who am I without X?" we ask, afraid the answer is no one or nothing.

Yes, you are leaping into the void, but it is a verdant void you leap into. In that void, new sides of yourself and your work will emerge. You are God's trapeze artist, partnered even as you leap into the air. It could be argued, "Leap and the net will appear" or even "Leap. God is the net." You will be caught, not caught up short. The risk you are taking is a worthy one.

It comes back to this idea: your creativity is a gift from God; your use of your creativity is your gift back to God. Every time you choose in favor of your creativity, you are choosing in favor of God. The phrase "God helps him who helps himself" will come to have rich meaning. As you move toward God, God moves toward you. When you place your creative nature first, you are placing God within you first. The "hole in the doughnut" may be revealed to be just the room that you needed in order to grow.

Dear X,

You are "between projects" and worried about never having another good idea.

Michelangelo told us his sculptures preexisted him. They were "locked in the marble," waiting to be freed. So it is for all of us. There are books, plays, songs, sculptures, art in all forms, waiting to come through us. Our job is to open ourselves to what would be created. Even when we do not know "how," we will be led a step at a time. It is in trusting the next step, the next word or brushstroke, that we artists exercise faith. Faith, when exercised, grows stronger like any other muscle.

Dear X,

I do not want you to panic. All artists go through dry spells—droughts, I call them, hoping to emphasize both that they are natural and that they will pass. The trick—and it is a "trick"—with a drought is to keep on keeping on. Morning writing stays in place. Creative excursions stay in place. Walks stay in place—if they can be said to stay in place. Perhaps the best thing to be said about walks is that they move us forward. For this reason, during a drought, I think walks should be doubled. It was St. Augustine who remarked, *"Solvitur ambulando."* Roughly translated, that means, "It is solved by walking." I find this to be true, especially as it relates to droughts. There is something in walking that limbers up our soul and not just our body. I often walk out with a problem and walk home with a solution. This can be a solution to a tricky creative problem or a personal one. You may have noticed that most of us turn instinctively to walking when we have something difficult to sort through. What I am suggesting to you is that you make your instincts conscious, that you deliberately "walk" through your drought.

I want to say something in favor of droughts: as painful as they are, they deepen us. When we feel we have "nothing to say" as artists, we are grappling with what it is we do want to say. In struggling to find our sources of inspiration, we find ourselves.

Another thing: a drought doesn't disqualify you as an artist. Rather, it is a rite of passage, an initiation period that while it pains us also makes us better. If we persist in making art even when we feel we have no art to make, we experience a deepened gratitude for those times when art comes to us more easily. In other words, droughts make us appreciate times of flow. As much as anything else, droughts teach us compassion for ourselves and others. Can this be anything but a blessing?

Dear X,

No, I don't mind your temper. I think it's a good thing, really. I know your drought feels like a dubious blessing at best, but I must ask you to trust me on this. One of the best books I ever wrote was also one of the most painful, written nearly entirely uphill during a period of self-doubt and self-loathing. By then I had been an artist for thirty years. I had gone through droughts before, although not as long and not as fierce. I had learned to "keep on keeping on" and so I took my own advice even though I didn't like it. Resistant, I wrote every morning. Resistant, I took creative excursions. Resistant, I went for walks. The walks I remember so clearly—beauty all around me and my stubborn fight against taking it in. Even remembering that drought makes me wince—and imagine my surprise and disbelief when the work done during it proved to be worthy, even fine?

I can almost hear you saying your drought is deeper, more stubborn, more killing than mine. Perhaps it is, but the same tools will still work to move you through it, and so I urge you not to abandon your tools or you will be abandoning yourself.

Dear X,

It sounds like your family is on a tear. In my experience, familial "concerns" are periodic, even seasonal. Every so often, it will occur to them, "Oh, dear, we ought to be worrying about X." (And they seem to have a positive genius for doing it when we feel at our most vulnerable.)

My family displayed an attitude I do not think is uncommon. On the one hand, they were proud to have an artist, a declared artist, in their ranks. On the other hand, they liked to act like such a scheme was half-baked, not nearly as sensible as their own choices. This let them enjoy the cachet of "guilt" by association, while still feeling comfortably secure in their own little niche. My cousins would take great pride at spotting one of my titles in a bookstore, and yet they would take great pride, too, that they weren't quite so "crazy" as to try a life in the arts.

What makes a life in the arts seem crazy? One thing: a lack of faith.

If life is about self-reliance, not God reliance, then avoiding a dream may seem pragmatic, something to be praised. If life is about God reliance, however, then half-measures avail us nothing. We must not only admit to our true dreams, we must have faith in their unfolding. In other words, if art is a vocation, and we are called, then we must also trust that by being true to ourselves, we will be cared for. After all, isn't it God who is doing the calling? That is certainly my perspective, and I have seen too many careers "work out" to doubt it.

Simply write your family, "I will be fine. Thanks for your concern, but all is well." Don't go into too many harrowing details with them, and their interest will fade. You will go back to being that interesting family oddity, "an artist."

Dear X,

So, cash and prizes! Congratulations on your grant. It is very nice to have your artist so honored. (And it does tend to quiet down the familial peanut gallery for a while, doesn't it?) The trick, of course, is to ignore the honor, not allow it to somehow raise the stakes, and go right on making art. (I am not trying to wet-blanket you by showing you the lead lining. I am just trying to save you some time, so bear with me.)

A film director friend of mine says the most difficult film to make is the second one. Why? Because of the attention that comes to you for the first. According to my friend, the anonymity of working when no one knows or cares you are working is an advantage. You are not, in his words, "distracted by success."

I think that the actual issue is one of self-consciousness. In order to work freely as artists, we must be able to forget ourselves. This happens when we are able to focus on the work moving through us rather than on us making the work. Any time our work is singled out either for praise or its opposite, we are vulnerable to feeling too self-conscious. We begin to work from our egos, not from our souls. This is why so many fine artists avoid reading their reviews. They have suffered— and I do mean suffered—from the aftershock. They have endured the self-consciousness of trying to work while with one eye watching themselves working. This is why, as artists, it behooves us always to focus on the art itself and not on ourselves as its maker. Perhaps so much glorious religious art got made because it was made anonymously. Certainly some of our finest art is made when our ego is the most submerged. Bach wrote weekly for his church—on assignment, as it were—and routinely wrote masterpieces. There is something about being in service to a greater whole—even "art" itself—that seems to set us free.

Dear X,

You write that your anger has you stalled in your tracks, too furious to function. I can't relate to that. To me, anger is fuel, and very usable fuel. This may sound petty, but I believe in making art "right at them." You knew your "friend" was a son of a bitch and he has just proved it, hopefully for the last time. Pin his rotten letter to the curtains where you work. Glance at it whenever you need a jolt of energy. You may be trying to be too "spiritual," to make art only from the loftiest of motives. Forget lofty motives, X. Make art from whatever is at hand. Don't wait to be in a good mood. That "good mood" may take a long time to happen. Instead, try working from precisely the mood you are in. Use your art to say "I feel this way about that—and right now." Think of your art as a time capsule. Allow it to capture exactly what and how you are feeling—and if that feeling is angry, then make angry art. Make art, not war. Art *is* the battleground.

Dear X,

What did you expect? Art is a form of alchemy. You cannot make angry art without that art transforming your anger into something else. You write that you made some angry art right at your rotten friend. You made a creativity totem to banish his negativity, and it is now banished. You write that you feel unexpectedly positive. Why "unexpected"? Don't tell me you are buying all that old propaganda about artists as dark and surly souls? I think "dark and surly" may belong more to blocked artists than to functional ones. In my experience, making art tends to make us more lighthearted—not shallow, just capable of life in some of the brighter keys. Why not enjoy your lighter moments?

Dear X,

You ask me if your commitment to making art makes you incapable of other commitments. To the contrary. Our commitment to our art trains us in the art of commitment. From it, we learn dailiness. We learn to just show up, setting aside our current mood. We learn to live one day at a time and we learn that each day builds one upon the next. Committed to our art, we learn to keep the drama on the page—or stage, or easel—and not place it where it doesn't belong, namely, in our relationship. Our commitment to art teaches us the value of consistency. It teaches us the value of longevity. It teaches us integrity, practicality, generosity. If we are willing to learn, there is very little our commitment to art can't teach us—and most especially in the realm of commitment. And so, yes, use your commitment to art as a model for your art of commitment. Did I say "Congratulations"? I think you will like "officially" living together.

Dear X,

Now you want to know how to manage to have "all of it." What a wonderful question, don't you think? In short, it is a balancing act. We balance our dreams against our days and we try to make progress in both. Frankly, however, I think dreams are practical. And I believe we can achieve more of our dreams than we may dare to believe—but it takes balance. It is hard, when you love something or someone, not to want to binge on them. Bingeing is just greediness and it is shortsighted. If I binge on my work today, I will be soured on it tomorrow. The same can be said of my romantic relationships. In an artful life, all is balance, and we are the ones who must find it.

You write that you love your work, you love your lover, and you wish for more hours in the day. So do we all. It is a learned trick, this idea that less may be more and that easy does it may be the best way to build something of worth. Not to be too facile, I might say artists tend to be extremists and so we must learn to be *extremely* balanced.

Have I said that I think you are well on your way to learning this trick? You are.

Dear X,

I could point out that you just got a grant, but I do not think that rationality has a lot to do with your current worries. Perhaps your newly minted domesticity is making you think ahead a little, projecting a few husbandly concerns, but of course "the money" bothers you. This is America. We are taught to think about life in monetary terms. We are taught to value our talents according to the financial return that they give us. But can talent really be quantified financially? Look at your hero, Vincent van Gogh. He was not a financially successful artist, yet who is more loved and revered? "Success" doesn't always come to us in worldly terms, as cash and prizes. Sometimes success is more intangible than that—a feeling of self-respect at living on our own terms, a sense of self-satisfaction at a job well done.

Many times, but not always, money does follow from doing what we love. In my case, I worked two decades to become an "overnight" success. In the decades since then, I have been well paid, but the real payoff, for me, has been the steadily growing body of work—and that has nothing to do with money. In fact, too much money can help to create too many diversions that keep us from doing our work. And so, as to money, it is good to have "enough," and enough may mean simply this: enough to live and work comfortably.

Your brother, you remind me, makes twice your income. Fine. Is your brother happy? Is he doing work he loves? You seem largely happy to me until you begin comparing. I think you should start to think of the urge to compare as a real demon for you. It seems to cause you that much trouble. Do you remember, a while back, when your cousins seemed to all be checking in? Remember how they were both proud of you and dubious about you? Remember how their doubt helped to stir up your own? Both doubt and faith can be encouraged by the company we keep. I would run your urge to compare yourself to your brother past your art buddy. That is a connection worth nurturing about which I hear all too little. Doesn't he have a few reservations about your comparisons too? I'll bet he does. For that matter, your lover wouldn't swap you for that brother of yours for an instant. Why not see if you can borrow a little loving loyalty and apply it to yourself?

Dear X,

Your news about your father is terrible. I am so sorry for your loss. You write that in your grief you do not feel like working. I can understand that—I just cannot cosign it as a course of conduct. Art is a very strong basket, my friend. It can hold whatever we ask it to bear, and that does not mean just our good times, our happiness. Some of the finest art is made from the harshest experience. Beethoven wrote more and more beautiful music as he grew deaf and could no longer hear it except in his mind's ear. Virginia Woolf fought bouts of madness and depression and forged her art in the midst of it. Artists lose parents, and lovers and children. We are not immune or exempt from the human condition. We may, however, have an added burden. We are asked not only to experience our lives but also to create art from the raw materials of our experience. In a sense, all artists lead lives twice—once as a participant and once as an objective observer, always asking, "What can be made from that?"

If I were to ask you to make art from your loss, you probably would label me a fanatic and a lunatic, but that is what I am suggesting to you. Rumi exploded into poetry when he lost his companion Sham. Out of that loss poured a fountain of art, a seemingly unstoppable flow. Pain was the catalyst for greatness and even for finding a path to further joy. I wish you the same consolation. Make art from your loss.

Dear X,

Good for you. I knew you would find some resilience and I am glad that you have. I agree with you that there is a strong dose of irony in working so well and knowing that your father will never see the work you have done. It is my mother, not my father, whom I lost young, and there have been many times when I have done work that I thought she would have been proud to have had me done. That is when it occurred to me that maybe she was more involved than simply "gone." We are the only culture I know of that doesn't worship ancestors in some form and that doesn't consider their ongoing guidance to be a reality. Maybe you should consider that now that he is on the other side, your father is finally getting his two cents in. It's possible.

Dear X,

It was good to get a letter from you again, although I was sorry to hear what generated it. You write that you are "not in the mood" to make art and that you haven't been for some time now. You wonder if it is possible to "lose" your vocation. I think it's a lot more possible to misplace it.

Most of the time, when my enthusiasm is dampened, there is no mystery. Something has dampened it. Often, the something is small and "shouldn't really" bother me. This is what I mean when I say artists are easily discouraged. We may be as strong as crabgrass, but that doesn't mean we can't be easily trodden underfoot. I'll give you a personal story. I had been working for some time on a project that I thought was a pretty good idea—good enough that I went to work every day with my tail wagging. Picture a golden retriever. You get the idea. My love for the project was so sunny, it made me a little blind to the dangers of the trail. Ignoring my usual rule about containment and about taking great care whom I first exposed a project to, I instead dashed off a longish letter to a friend of mine, full of the project and my plans for it. A week went by. Then two. I didn't get a letter back from my friend nor did I get a phone call. My project began to seem mysteriously less interesting. I began to have to push myself to work on it. Its central idea—the one I'd been so crazy about—began to seem a bit muddy to me. Amnesia struck. I couldn't remember exactly why the project had ever seemed like a good one. In fact, I was tempted to abandon it altogether—a far cry from my prior joyous productivity—and that's when I remembered the telltale letter.

I mention all of this in the hope that a little searching on your part will turn up a similar culprit. Meanwhile, let me say this: I am hard at work on a very interesting project that I am *not* talking about.

Dear X,

No, I am not a genius, but I am very glad you were able to pull your thorn from your paw. It is so often true that just the smallest bit of sleuthing will show us a wound that has infected us with discouragement. So many wounds happen in passing and we really do not notice them—not until their poison has done its work and we are mysteriously sickened. We need to take particular care with our creative companions. Discouragement is contagious—perhaps especially when it comes to the door dressed as "realism."

I have a very "realistic" friend whom I now avoid like the plague. A writer who is not writing very much, this friend is full of bad news about the state of publishing: shrinking advances, the sorry plight of midlist fiction, the dearth of "real" editors. Now, everything this writer says is true enough, but it ignores the essential fact that if you write well enough and often enough, you may very well continue to be well published. Why is it there are no panels convening to break to us the good news? I think we may need to find that for ourselves, and perhaps professional artists' groups are not the ideal place to go looking. For myself, I like to keep the spectrum of my friendships varied. I find that nonwriters have a great deal to recommend them—chief among them, perhaps, their enthusiasm about writing itself.

Once a week, on Tuesdays, I dine with a nonwriting friend.

I hear a good dose of the nonwriting world and I often come home with a fine writer's lesson to apply to life. My friend is a quilter. This already takes more patience than I can imagine and yet, as my wondering eyes behold, her daily practice of "just showing up and doing what I can" results in entire quilts. Quilts that end up in museums and private collections. Quilts that have made my friend quite well known in "quilting" circles. To my eye, she is quite literally that estimable thing, a "fine artist." Perhaps because I make them, books do not seem so miraculous. To my quilting friend, on the other hand, my writer's life is a thing of magic and mystery. Our mutual admiration has held up through two decades of work and tonight I have dinner with her again. I wish you more friends like her.

Dear X,

That's wonderful news about your young neighbor-protégée. For some time now, I have been thinking you needed someone to talk to in just the same way I have talked to you. It's good for us, this business of the oral tradition. What is it they say? You have to give it away to keep it? Well, it is time for you to start giving it away, and it sounds like you have found some willing ears. Let me know how it goes. Mentoring is a tricky business.

This morning I got a letter from a writer I admire. He was "back on the page" after a month away, a pause occasioned by a sudden illness in his family. He writes that he thinks writing is a *grieving* process. I know what he means, but I would say making art is a *cherishing* process, a slightly more upbeat way of putting it. I think we use art to caress what our consciousness notices and is interested by. For example, my writing desk looks out across rooftops, not quite Currier and Ives scale but still charming. I get a great swath of sky and a view of my neighbors, slightly miniaturized, leading their lives. At Christmas, I see into living rooms festooned with brightly lit trees and I sense this greater life we are all sharing.

You mention that your walks have drawn you more deeply into life. Like me, you take in the cats in the windows, the Christmas trees or holiday boughs, the sense that we are all part of some grand stew. Myself, I like being an ingredient amid ingredients. I hope I bring to life some spice and savor.

Have I said to you that you do? It has been a pleasure and a privilege, this exchange of ideas with you. I am grateful to you for inaugurating it and, I guess, I look to you to pass it on, an oral tradition, artist to artist. I believe we are all tutored by a higher hand, and that as we are open to it, opportunities and blessings come to us. You have been one of my blessings. I hope I have been one of your opportunities.

Walking in This World
Practical strategies for creativity
Julia Cameron

Take the next step on the path to discovering your true potential. Instead of resisting yourself, try finding yourself irresistible.

In her international bestseller, *The Artist's Way*, Julia Cameron created a course cherished by millions of aspiring and working artists. *Walking in This World* is the long-awaited sequel that picks up where *The Artist's Way* left off. This groundbreaking new book offers a second course in creative discovery – Part Two in an amazing journey towards unlocking our human potential.

Walking in This World is packed with valuable strategies and techniques that will enable you to:

- create with ease, letting your work flow
- overcome the blocks that come from either too few or too many ideas
- refresh your enjoyment in your work and your life
- connect with inspiration and your inner creative spirit
- learn how to deal with criticism from within or outside

A profoundly inspired work by the leading authority on the subject of creativity, *Walking in This World* is destined to become a true classic.

Buy Rider Books

Order further Rider titles from your local bookshop, or have them delivered direct to your door by Bookpost

Walking in This World by Julia Cameron	£12.99
Flow: The Psychology of Happiness by Mihaly Csikszentmihalyi	£10.99
Women Who Run With The Wolves by Clarissa Pinkola Estes	£12.99
Focusing by Eugene T. Gendlin	£7.99
Intuition & Beyond by Sharon A. Klingler	£7.99
Secrets & Mysteries by Denise Linn	£9.99
Emotional Alchemy by Tara Bennett-Goleman	£8.99
The Little Book of Bliss by Patrick Whiteside	£2.50
The Little Book of Inner Space by Stafford Whiteaker	£2.50
The Little Book of Blue Thoughts by Rabbi Lionel Blue	£2.50

FREE POST AND PACKING
Overseas customers allow £2.00 per paperback

ORDER:
By phone: 01624 677237

By post: Random House Books
c/o Bookpost
PO Box 29
Douglas
Isle of Man, IM99 1BQ

By fax: 01624 670923

By email: bookshop@enterprise.net

Cheques (payable to Bookpost) and credit cards accepted

Prices and availability subject to change without notice.
Allow 28 days for delivery.
When placing your order, please state if you do not wish to receive
any additional information.

www.randomhouse.co.uk